Humblebee
Bumblebee

HUMBLEBEE BUMBLEBEE

*The life story of the
friendly bumblebees and their use
by the backyard gardener*

by
BRIAN L. GRIFFIN
illustrated by the author

First Edition 1997; (2nd printing in 2000)
Knox Cellars Publishing, Bellingham, Washington USA
E-mail: brian@knoxcellars.com
Website: http://www.knoxcellars.com

Grateful acknowledgment is made to Logaston Press for
permission to reprint previously published material from
The Humblebee, by F.W.L. Sladen. Copyright 1989.

Library of Congress Cataloging-in Publication Data pending

Griffin, Brian L.

Includes bibliographical references and field guide to North
American bumblebees.

Cover painting by Brian L. Griffin
Design/Composition: Kathleen R. Weisel

ISBN: number 0-9635841-3-8

Printed in the United States of America

Acknowledgments

The author expresses his gratitude to the following persons whose skills and assistance made this book happen.

Dr. Lynn Royce, entomologist at Oregon State University, Corvallis, Oregon, for her interest and affection for the bumblebees, for her encouragement and help and especially for showing me how to capture bumblebee colonies.

Dr. Stephen Buchmann, entomologist with the United States Department of Agriculture at the Bee Laboratory in Tucson, Arizona, and co-author of *The Forgotten Pollinators,* for his dedication to telling the story of our continent's pollinators and for his help in reviewing this manuscript for technical accuracy.

Beverly Johanson who once again had the patience and goodness to use her English teacher skills in correcting and critiquing my literary efforts.

My daughter and partner Lisa Griffin Novich, whose gentle insistence that I must write this book finally got me past that peculiar inhibition, writer's block.

Finally I would like to acknowledge those long deceased naturalists and writers of an earlier century, J. Henre Fabre and F.W.L. Sladen whose unique gifts of observation and communication have brought the excitement and wonders of the natural world to me and to so many others through their wonderfully crafted books.

Dedication

To my grandchildren

Evan, Annie, Kyle, Katherine, Laura, and Drew

who, with their innate curiosity and enthusiasm, inspire me to continue telling the story of pollination and our native bees so that they and others can share in the wonders of the natural world and find in it the motivation to become lifetime learners. To them I dedicate this little book in the hope that they will always remember the joy of learning that we have shared.

Contents

Illustrations

Foreword

It has always seemed strange to us that so little has been written by North Americans about the bumble-bee. No insect is more familiar to us. With the possible exception of the ladybug, no insect is more fondly regarded, and surely few insects are more beneficial to mankind's efforts to make a living on this continent. Most of the rather sparse literature available to the non-academic world about bumblebees has come from England, and much of that very many years ago. That is not to say that because a book is very old and of English origin it is not of value.

Quite to the contrary, the quintessential book about bumblebees was written in 1912 by the British amateur naturalist F.W.L. Sladen. His book still reads with charm and excitement and its information, for the most part, has withstood the assaults of time and scientific investigation.

Sladen's first book about bumblebees was written twenty years earlier, in 1892, when he was but a lad of sixteen. It was the first book about bumblebees in the English language and perhaps in any language and Sladen entitled it *The Humble Bee, Its Life History & How To Domesticate It.* He handwrote it, illustrated it and then printed his juvenile treatise on a stenciling machine. The little book sold for six pence and it earned young Sladen the attention and astonished praise of those interested in "humble" bees at the time.

His publication of 1912 which carried the same title is a mature elaboration on what the youthful Sladen had begun. Sladen wrote in a pleasing and hospitable fashion which allows a reader, even today, to read his book with pleasure and understanding. It remains remarkably accurate and correct even in the face of the decades of study of the bumblebee since 1912.

Perhaps the American bumblebee classic is O.E. Plath's *Bumblebees and Their Ways* published in 1934. It too enjoys the blessing of readability. We commend both of them to you, dear reader. You might get lucky and find copies in your public library or, failing that, a good university library will surely have them. Happily, Sladen's great classic was re-published in 1989 by Logaston Press of Herefordshire, England. It is distributed by Northern Bee Books, Scout Bottom Farm, Mytholmroyd, Hebden Bridge, Yorkshire U.K. HX7 5JS. (ISBN 0 9510242 3X). We recommend it as a fine addition to your library.

Despite the quality of the books of Sladen and Plath we think it is time for another bumblebee book, one that is scientifically accurate but entertaining and pleasant to read. As the twentieth century draws to a close North America faces a pollination crisis of yet unknown dimensions because of the plague of mites and diseases that reduce our honeybee populations. Agricultural insecticide and herbicide practices that completely ignore the needs of insect pollinators worsen the problem. In addition North Americans are rapidly becoming an urbanized people losing touch with the natural world and its creatures.

We at Knox Cellars are pleased that Brian Griffin, the author of *The Orchard Mason Bee*, a charming and information-filled book about another North American pollinating bee, has broadened his field of interest to include our many species of bumblebees and has written this informative and entertaining *Humblebee Bumblebee*. We hope that through this book the peoples of this continent will become familiar with its native bumblebees and recognize their great value. We hope that North Americans will learn from this book to protect all bees and to propagate bumblebees in their urban and rural gardens in order to help reverse the tragic decline of pollinating bees on our continent.

Preface

Surely everyone knows the great furry bumblebee, that gentle giant of the blossoms, that somehow awkward, slow, bumbling bear of a bee. Were not your childhood summers marked by the friendly buzz of this wonderful creature that assures us of a bountiful crop of raspberries each year, that amazes us with its sheer immensity each spring, and amuses us with its slow and rumbling flight?

Of course you know of its important role in pollinating the world around us. You must be familiar with the old saw about the prominent aeronautical engineer who pronounced flight impossible for a bumblebee, her sheer weight and mass too great to be borne aloft by her tiny wings?

Surely every child has had the heady experience of catching a foraging bumblebee in an old Mason jar, of feeling its resonant and angry buzz vibrate through the metal lid, and then, realizing that delicious excitement of indecision, hesitate to lift the lid to release the bee, fearing some angry retaliation for its brief imprisonment.

I have thought that these were the common experiences, but to my surprise and sorrow the reality is quite different. I find many people who don't seem to know just what a bumblebee looks like, others who assure me that they are terrified of bumblebees or any bee for that matter. These people are often quick to kill any colonies of bumblebees with poison sprays, ignoring the very peaceful nature of almost all bees and the crucial role they play in nature's scheme. Other folks ask, "Just what are bumblebees good for anyway?" apparently having no idea what role nature planned for this invaluable long-tongued pollinator.

As for the aeronautical engineer who pronounced the bumblebee flightless, well—his ignorance needs no comment.

The purpose, then, of this little book is to dispel some of the myths and mists that surround this gentle creature and to spread the word about the life and works of that great subfamily of the bumblebees called *Bombinae*

You may be wondering how I came to be interested in the bumblebee at all. Unlike the story of Adam and Eve, which began with an apple, my story began with the lack of apples. Ten years ago I planted a Belgian fence along the western border of our back yard. "Belgian Fence" is the term for a fence of fruit trees planted close together along a wall or fence line and trained in the espalier (es-pal-yeh) method to grow in a formal and symmetrical design.

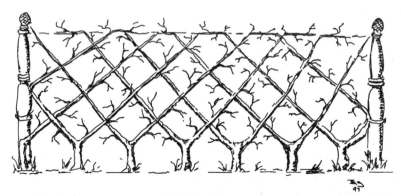

Belgian Fence

My fence consists of fifty-two apple and pear trees planted two and one-half feet apart and trained to grow shaped like the letter Y. Each of the arms of the Y cross and cross again with the arms of its neighboring tree in a lattice-like fashion. The fence was a huge esthetic success but I was not getting much fruit. The culprit I eventually learned was poor pollination.

By chance I learned about a native pollinating bee called the Orchard Mason Bee (*Osmia lignaria*) and began propagating them. My fate was sealed. I was increasingly fascinated as I peered deeper and deeper into the world of our native bees. I propagated more and more Orchard Masons and soon I was selling my excess bees. Then I was compelled to write my first book *The Orchard Mason Bee* and with its immediate acceptance among nature lovers I found myself in demand as a speaker.

What had begun as a hobby became something more. I was fascinated by the variety and sheer numbers of species of our native bees. The more I learned about the bees the more I realized how little I knew and how much there was to learn.

Then a few years ago North America was invaded by a pair of mites which began decimating the European honeybee population in the South. As the scourge swept north the alarm rang across the country: "We are losing our honeybees, what will we do for pollination?"

The questions came to me in many ways: from customers' inquiries, by letter and phone, at every speaking engagement, and people stopped me on the street. "What will we do for pollination?" was their concerned plaint. The answer was so obvious and the need to tell the story seemed so great.

North America is blessed with a host of native bees over four thousand separate species. They were here pollinating our continent long before the colonists brought their European honeybees to Jamestown almost four hundred years ago. We have ignored those native pollinators in large part, but they are still here in uncounted numbers doing their essential job. We know enough to know that if we provide them with habitat and opportunity, many of them can be even better pollinators than their cousins, the European honey bees.

I began watching the great bumblebees that joined my Orchard Masons feeding on the *Pieris japonica* shrub in the spring. Those huge specimens of the early spring seemed to give way to many more but smaller bumblebees as spring turned into summer and my berries and vegetables blossomed. I wondered what had happened to those large bees and where their smaller imitations had come from. I began to read about the bumblebee and attempted to assemble all of the literature that I could find. I was amazed to learn that the bees could be attracted to and propagated in wooden houses just like the violet green swallows we have encouraged to nest in our yard each spring.

Soon I had a conversation with Lynn Royce, an Oregon State University entomologist who had been interested in my work with Orchard Mason bees. Lynn revealed that she was a lover of bumblebees and she invited me to Corvallis to tour the OSU entomology department, to use their fine library and, best of all, to help her capture a bumblebee colony of my own.

Lynn responds to the "help" calls that come to the university from people who find a colony of bees living closer than they find comfortable. On her own time she rescues the bumblebees, removing the colony to a safe place where they are no longer a bother to the caller.

She called me one July morning to report that she had a nice colony of *Bombus californicus* nesting in an old mouse nest in a woodpile north of Corvallis. Would

I like to come and get it? I was on the road the next day. The three hundred miles to Corvallis seemed a small price to pay for such an opportunity.

As I drove home I realized that I was hopelessly enamored of the bumblebee. I brought back with me a nest box occupied by lovely black and yellow bees, a head swimming with new-found knowledge and practical experience, and the germ of an idea to write another book about bees.

Here, then is the result of my recent experiences with bumblebees, but most of its content has been gleaned from the works of such pioneers in bumblebee research as Sladen, Franklin and Plath. It is my sincere hope that it will inspire you to know the bumblebee better and to respect its needs for habitat in the part of this earth that you inhabit. It is my special hope that you will establish nesting colonies in your own yard that you can observe and learn from and, most importantly, use to teach others about this marvelous and beneficial insect.

Chapter One

The Life Story of the Bumblebees

The late February day dawned clear and cool. For the first time in months there was a mildness in the air.

The rising sun began to warm the earth and as it did so, life began to stir in the torpid body lying in a tiny chamber several inches under the surface. Little by little, as the earth warmed about it, the sleeping bee also warmed. Soon, with ever-quickening movements, she was wide awake and ready to dig her way out of the entrance tunnel she had dug to her hibernaculum the previous August.

For six months she had been hibernating, curled into a heat-saving ball, slowly metabolizing the fat reserves stored in her robust body. Now she would emerge

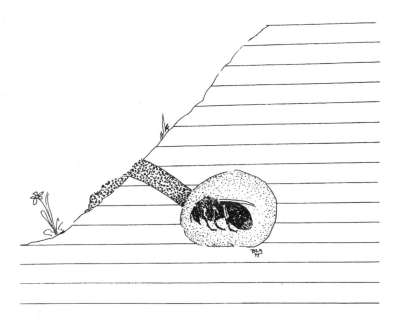

Queen in the Hiberculum

to the sunlight to start a new cycle in the wondrous life of the bumblebee.

Facing the still soft earth of the entrance tunnel, she began to dig with her front legs like a dog, passing dirt between her two sets of rear legs. She dug upward following the tunnel tailings she had left behind the previous summer. Finally she burst out into the dimly remembered daylight. A ravenous hunger possessed her and she hurriedly groomed her wings for flight. Soon the warm February sun had warmed her to flight temperature and she took wing in search of energy-giving nectar.

In my garden she and other queens like her find it in the urn-like hanging blossoms of a huge *Pieris japonica* shrub whose new blossoms lure them with their honeyed scent. She drinks her fill using her long tongue to great advantage. A new cycle of bumblebee life has begun. Soon she will be joined by others: her sisters of the same and other species, each of them entirely alone in the world, all of them bearing the promise of a new bumblebee colony and the future of their race in the sexual organs of their bodies.

These huge early bees are the foundress queens who are charged by Mother Nature with establishing a new colony of bumblebees. It is a heavy responsibility. The entire future of the bumblebee race depends on the success of these gravid queens. Every other member of their colony of the previous summer perished with the onset of winter. The only goal of all of those now-dead ancestors was to prepare new queens to carry on the species the following spring. In preparation for her mission each of the foundress queens mated the previous summer just before digging her way into the hibernation chamber, (the hibernaculum). In her special organ, the spermatheca, the semen from that mating resides having waited through the long winter to be used during the egg-laying process.

Before the egg laying can begin our now fed and re-energized queen must find a proper home in which to build her colony. She and other queens will search back and forth, over woodlots and grasslands, looking for that perfect spot. She might take up to three weeks to find that place, feeding on nectar for energy and spending the night clinging to a leaf or twig. This is a dangerous time for the queens as there are many other creatures hungry from the long cold winter and lusting for protein to build back their own strength for the nesting frenzy awaiting their species. Rapacious birds lurk everywhere, just waiting the chance for a tasty bee lunch. Spiders search the branches and leaves for juicy feasts while our foundress queen searches only for a perfect home.

Finally the eager queen finds the perfect place, an abandoned mouse nest tucked deep into an opening in a woodpile of sawed branches stacked under a large walnut tree. As she has many times before, she slowly flies by examining it carefully. She passes by again and again. Finally she lands on a branch just before the nest and investigates on foot. This is the place. The outer surface is made of leaves, bits of grass, twigs and pieces of string that the previous occupant and builder picked up. She crawls inside and finds fine grasses and thistledown, and best of all, hair from the mother mouse to provide fine warm insulation.

All of our queen's requirements are met. The nest is dark, secluded, protected from the elements, and filled with warm insulating material. She crawls in, busily pulls material about herself and, with her own body warmth, begins to dry out the nesting material.

Each of her kind will find a similar place, some in mouse nests dug into the ground, some in the insulation provided by an old mattress tossed aside in a shed, some in the feathered warmth of an abandoned bird house. I have even heard of a colony of bumblebees which nested in a mouse nest in an abandoned teapot lying in the corner of a garden. Yes, they used the spout for an entrance and exit portal.

Teapot Home.

There are dozens of different species of bumblebees to be found in North America. There are many different life styles to be found among them. Some of the species are predominately underground nesters seeking field mouse burrows. Some species prefer to find a mouse nest just above the earth in a clump of grasses, while others are quite content high up in a birdhouse or in the attic insulation of a house. What does seem generally true is that bumblebees usually don't construct their own nest by searching and bringing in materials. They are content to re-arrange found nesting materials where they find them.

As soon as a queen finds the perfect home she carefully fixes its location in her memory. When she leaves her new home for the first time she embarks on a series of locating flights. She turns around and observes the nest for a bit, then slowly rises into the air and flies a series of gradually widening circles with her head turned toward the nest entrance. Then, apparently confident that she has the location memorized, she flies off about her business. For the next few times that she leaves the nest she again takes several orienting flight circles, but with each exit she grows more confident of her navigation until finally she just flies straight off, sure that she can find her way home.

Once our foundress queen has arranged and dried the nesting materials to her liking and lived in her new abode for a few days she begins to get "broody." This old fashioned term was used to describe the moody fussiness apparent in chickens when they were getting in the mood to lay eggs and start a family. It applies to bumblebees as well.

She makes a small cavity near the center of the nesting material and now she spends much of her time in the nest with her body pressed gently against the floor of the cavity. Her body heat continues to warm and dry the nesting material. Glands between her abdominal segments begin to secrete wax, and she takes care to leave the nest when flying conditions are good to consume large quantities of nectar necessary in producing the wax. The wax is pressed out between the plates of the abdominal segments and take the form of tiny waxen shingles.

She removes the "shingles" with her feet and brings them to her mandibles to be chewed into usable shapes that are then applied to her construction projects. When the amount of waxen shingles has reached the proper accumulation she constructs a honey pot near the inner doorway of her home and she fills the honey pot with nectar for use during the night or when the weather is so inclement that she cannot forage.

The Honey Pot.

The honey pot is rather different in size and structure between the species but it is essentially a waxen cup, open at the top and placed within reach of the queen as she sits on her brood. It enables her to sip nectar during the long hours that she will brood her young.

The honey pot is built at the entrance to the nesting chamber so that she may face the entrance and guard against intruders while still enjoying its convenience and comfort. When the honey pot is built and provisioned with regurgitated nectar, she begins her egg capsule.

Centered on the floor of the nesting cavity she fashions a tiny cup of wax. This cup is about the size of a pencil eraser. When the queen is ready she inserts the tip of her abdomen into the cup, which she holds with her third pair of legs, and she lays about eight eggs into it. As each egg is laid, her sting penetrates the wall of the cell. Some observers think that the sting helps steady the cup and is an aid to egg laying, but no one really knows for sure.

A wax covering or canopy is constructed over the freshly laid eggs so that the eggs are in a tiny waxen capsule. In three or four days the eggs hatch into larvae. As the larvae grow under their waxen canopy, their growth can be noted by the ever larger lumps which appear under the blanket.

The bee youngsters must be fed. Sladen believed that the egg cell is built on top of a lump of pollen which is later eaten by the larvae. Others report that queens deposit pollen into the cell after the eggs are laid, while still others report that the queens feed all of their larvae by regurgitation. It may be that all of these methods are utilized but by different bumblebee species. It is sure that in some species the queen will now and then open the waxen envelope and, with several contractions of her abdomen, regurgitate a yellowish liquid, probably a mixture of pollen and honey, into the envelope. The larvae greedily devour it while the queen repairs the rent in the cup covering.

In other species, special pockets are built onto the sides of the cup holding the larvae, and pollen is sealed into those pockets. The larvae access and consume the pollen by penetrating the inner wall of their cell.

The larvae grow very rapidly on the rich diet foraged by their mother. As the larvae grow, the queen constantly rebuilds and adds to the nest capsule in order to accommodate the brood's growth. The eight pairs of wax-producing glands are now working at peak production.

Queen in the Nesting Chamber

She has thus far spent all of her time, when not foraging, brooding her larvae like a setting hen, lying upon the egg cluster with her abdomen greatly distended and her legs grasping the sides of the waxen envelope.

The warmth pumped through her body, combined with her weight, causes the growing egg cluster to sag in the center and rise higher at the sides, thus forming a groove in which the queen lies while incubating the brood.

About seven days after hatching from the egg, the larvae spin cocoons about themselves and soon transform into pupae. From this point until they emerge as adults, they need no more food. The affection of the queen seems to increase as the pupae develop and she leaves the cocoons only to provide a bit of food for herself during the remaining days of development. She is usually found spreading herself as broadly as possible over the cocoons of her growing babies, her abdomen busily pulsing as her warm blood is pumped through her abdomen to warm the pupae.

The incubating larvae and pupae are very sensitive to cold. If the brood is chilled, or suffers from lack of food, the duration of the pre-adult stages may be extended or, indeed, the infants may die. If all has gone well the adult bees will emerge about twenty-two days after the eggs were laid. Those in the maternal groove, presumably the beneficiaries of more warmth, usually mature a couple of days before the young on the edge of the pupal envelope.

The young workers are usually assisted in cutting out of their golden cocoons by their mother, and the first workers to emerge are soon helping their sisters cut their way to freedom. It is proper to say sisters because all of this first brood will be females, made of that gender when the queen fertilized the egg at its laying with a bit of the semen stored in her spermatheca. The colony cannot afford the luxury of producing males, whose only role is a reproductive one, until it is well populated and prosperous. As a result all of the broods are female workers until late in the season.

The newly emerged workers are much smaller than the queen, their size reduced by meager nourishment due to the queen's inability to forage for food and keep them warm at the same time. Later generations of workers will become larger and larger as the colony becomes more prosperous and food foraging can be done by its ever-growing numbers of workers.

For now, the queen's first assistants are rather small and of a silvery white color. It takes about three days for the workers to adopt the ancestral dress of black and yellow or red, and to reach full color. Immediately upon emerging, the silvery white pile is matted against

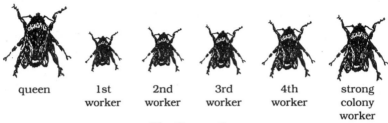

| queen | 1st worker | 2nd worker | 3rd worker | 4th worker | strong colony worker |

The Generations

the black bodies of the bees and they bear little resemblance to the rich velvety creatures they will become. Their first act upon emergence is to clean their legs and antennae. Then to the honey pot to drink deeply of the nectar. Soon their pile becomes dry and velvety and their wings, moist and curved around their bodies at emergence, become straight and hard.

In two or three days their wings are strong enough for flight. The coat has turned the color of the species and our new workers are ready to venture into the field and begin their life's labors.

When the larvae of the first brood spun their cocoons the queen, pressed by the instinct to increase, constructed another tiny cup and attached it to the side of the growing original egg cluster. In it she laid another batch of eight eggs, covering them with their waxen cover, and in several days she did it again.

By the time her first eggs hatched into workers she had three additional broods in differing stages of development, all attached to the original egg cluster. The comb structure has begun.

Now she has eight helpers who can feed the larvae, help incubate the larval clumps and, most importantly, forage for pollen and nectar to feed the growing family. When the colony is going at full tilt the queen might be laying eggs every day, and the frantic activity of feeding, foraging, incubating, and constructing finds furry bees running every which way inside the colony.

Egg-laying cups are always added to the shoulder of a developing larval clump. The queen will never lay her eggs in a used pupal case, only in a new cup which she constructs of wax, and so the structure of the colony grows and grows, ever upward. As bees emerge from the pupal cocoons, the cocoons are frequently converted to the storage of pollen or nectar. More often they are simply abandoned to be used as underpinnings of the growing colony.

The colony takes on the form of a medieval castle with turrets and domes ever rising, built upon the cocoon structure of the immediately preceding batch of workers. Down in the dungeons in the bottom of the colony will be found storage cocoons filled with pollen reserves. The golden cocoons which had their tops cut out by the emerging bees will sometimes be filled with pollen and then capped over with brown wax.

Some of the open-topped cocoons toward the top of the colony will have their sides extended with wax and be filled with nectar. A large and growing colony will have a number of open-topped honey pots to feed its hard working population. If times are very prosperous and more nectar is collected than can be used in the day-to-day life of the colony, the water from the nectar in the cocoons is evaporated and the nectar gradually turns into honey and those cells are capped with wax for storage.

Bumblebee honey is much thicker than honeybee honey. It is reputed to be excellent in taste, richer and more flavorful than honeybee honey. O.E. Plath, in a charming introduction to his book *Bumblebees And Their Ways,* cites the discovery that bumblebees make

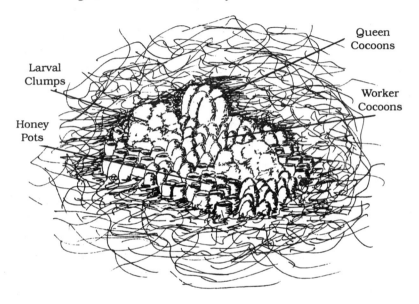

Medieval Castle

delicious honey as the foundation for his interest in bumblebees. During his childhood in Central Europe he began collecting bumblebee colonies and transferring them to his home so as to "have honey available at all times"

Bumblebee wax is less exotic than honeybee wax. It is rather darker brown and has less hardness and substance; nevertheless it is a precious commodity in a bumblebee society. The bees use the wax again and again. It is taken from an old structure to build up the sides of a storage cocoon or to cover over a freshly laid clutch of eggs. Certainly its most dramatic use is to build a canopy over the entire colony so that looking at its top is like looking at a round brown baseball.

This very effective temperature control device takes huge resources of wax but is within the capability of a healthy colony because the workers, like the queen, also secrete wax from their abdominal glands.

Inventive uses of wax shields have also been observed. In a small colony of *Bombus californicus* that I had living in an observation box in my workshop, the bees built a shield wall in front of the entrance hole to the nesting chamber. They had lived without such a shield for over a month during warm weather, but when a few days of cold weather came along they began construction. Using upholsterer's cotton on the outside and a thin skin of wax on the inside, they built a wall just high enough to shield a developing cluster of pupal cells that were directly in front of the entrance hole.

Those cells were no doubt getting a cool draft from the entrance chamber. The structure looked for all the world like a piece of a tennis ball attached to the comb with rubber on the inside and woolly nap on the outside. When the weather warmed again, the bees ceased construction.

The comb continues to expand as the colony matures and grows, taking more and more room in the nest cavity. If the colony is prosperous enough the comb may completely fill the available space in the nesting box or container. Then, says Sladen, the oldest cocoons at the bottom of the comb are bitten down and the entire comb sinks onto its collapsed foundations providing new construction space at the top.

As the comb increases in size the bees frequently need more insulating nesting material. Plath reports that some species accomplish this by collecting dried grass and moss that they find near the nest. He describes observing them usually in the evening after most of the workers have returned from the field. As many as twenty of the workers were seen within a foot of their home. "Facing away from the nest each worker seizes a bit of moss or dry grass in her mandibles and passes it beneath her body to the third pair of legs, which push the fragment as far as possible in the direction of the nest. A worker nearer to the nest then seizes this material and treats it in the same manner." Finally the nest is re-supplied with insulating material.

The great work of the bumblebee worker class is the collection of nectar and pollen. Not infrequently, after successfully establishing her colony, the queen will no longer leave it. She is too busy laying eggs, feeding the young, and doing her other homely duties. All of the food gathering becomes the responsibility of the workers. Very good at their task of gathering both nectar and pollen on the same trip, they will frequently visit different pollen and nectar sources, mixing their gatherings from various blossoms into the communal storage containers.

Pollen is gathered in the specialized hairs on their legs commonly called "pollen baskets" while the nectar is swallowed into their honey stomach. Upon their return to the colony the worker bees pass over the storage cocoons and regurgitate the contents of the honey stomach into it. Then, finding a pollen storage cocoon, they stand on the edge facing away from the cocoon and insert their hind legs carrying the pollen down into the cocoon. With a rapid, slicing downward movement of the middle pair of legs, they remove the pollen from the pollen baskets on their legs. Then they are off for another load.

The life of the worker bumblebee is not an easy one. They are easily as industrious as the fabled honeybee. If the weather is warm enough, bumblebees will begin to forage before dawn and they frequently are still hard at work after the sun has gone down. Their life is spent in almost ceaseless work. When the day's foraging is over the bees can be observed scurrying around the comb busy with their various duties.

As a result of this workaholic existence their life span is only about a month. Their lustrous pile, so colorful and rich in youth, is soon worn and faded. The wings become tattered and ragged about the edges and finally, unable to complete a foraging trip, the exhausted bee dies, alone and unmourned.

Both the individual bee and the colony as a whole have a single ultimate purpose: the continuation of their species through the production of the sexual castes. Late in the life of the colony the queen will lay both queen and male eggs. If enough of these sexually charged late-comers survive to maturity; if they successfully mate; and if the young mated queens live through the winters hibernation, they will assure the survival of the species to the next spring.

It is difficult to assign a date to the demise of a bumblebee colony for each species has its own season. It is accurate to say that all bumblebees delay the production of their sexual players, males and new queens, until late in the life of their individual colony.

Some bumblebee species begin colony building in February and are through with their cycle of life in two months. Bumblebees in the high arctic must complete their life cycles in two weeks. Many species survive well into October.

When the colony is ready, the tiring queen lays egg clusters that are destined to be males and queens.

Sladen said "it is virtually impossible to distinquish male brood from worker brood." However there can be no doubt about the queen cells. They are huge in comparison to worker and male cocoons. Sometimes a cluster will contain both male and queen cocoons although as a rule, egg clusters contain but one gender.

It is a simple matter to explain the laying of a male egg. It is an egg that the queen does not fertilize with semen from its spermatheca. Female worker eggs have been fertilized by the semen from the previous summer's matings, but what of queen eggs? They are not so easy to explain. Is it simply a worker egg that is fed differently? Is a special hormone contributed by the old queen to create the new queens? It is not known for sure how queen eggs are created but created they are. The resulting large pupae take longer to attain their full size than either the worker or male pupae.

Perhaps twice as many males as queens are created. The males, when they emerge, almost immediately leave the colony never to return. They appear to idle about sleeping on thistle heads. Actually the bumblebee males are anything but idle. They are busily establishing and patrolling sexual "traplines" which are baited with scent. The males patrol these "traplines" relentlessly day after day. Their goal of course is to attract a new queen to one of their scented "trap" locations where breeding will occur.

As the males are placing and maintaining their lures, the new queens are emerging. Beautiful and fulsome, they spend a few days gaining their full color, preparing their wings for flight, and even doing a little work around the comb. But when they have reached their full maturity, when their coat is luxuriant and rich, they leave the colony for good.

Now it is late August, or mid September or, for a few species, even early October. Now is the time for the culmination of the bumblebees' destiny. The old queen lies trembling and weak in the colony that she founded and ruled for so long. Her worker children, tattered and faded lie dying about her, the various vermin that always attack the dwindling nest are eating away at the foundations and stores of her comb castle, but her latest progeny are outside the nest, seeking a rendezvous with survival—survival of their race.

Males and females must find each other to assure another year of blessings for the earth. They must find each other and mate to assure that the berries and trees and crops of North America will be pollinated and can recreate their own.

In that annual miracle of nature the males and females do meet and mate, and the way that they find each other is marvelous indeed. We have mentioned that the males set up a "trapline" baited with scent. Each male establishes a closed loop circuit baited at intervals with his male attractant scent. The scent is placed on a rose bush here, a fence post a bit farther along. Every several yards he leaves a bit of chemical that is calculated to attract the females.

His circuit may be several hundred feet in length and he patrols it for all his waking hours. His "trapline" is crossed and intersected by dozens of the "traplines" of other eager males each flying their circuits hoping to find a willing queen at one of their "traps."

If the mating "traplines" were visible from above the earth you would be looking down at a never-ending pattern of overlapping circuits, each with an eager male bumblebee flying around and around it. Now into this web of intrigue enters one of our newly emerged virgin queens.

She flies about the countryside, stopping at first one, then two amorously scented flowers or leaves, but no one is there to greet her. Then as she arrives at a

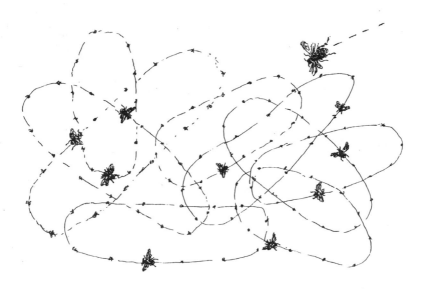

Mating Circuits

third tempting pavilion she is greeted by a male who has just arrived himself. A brief coupling occurs and now our former virgin flies on. She may stop at any number of scent stations and be met and bred by any number of males as she wanders the countryside.

After a bit she tires of these dalliances and her thoughts turn to the long winter ahead. The now gravid queen turns her attention to finding her winter's resting chamber. On a north-facing bank, in well drained soil, she digs her hibernaculum. She tunnels into the soft cool earth—digging with her front legs and passing the dirt behind her through her rear sets of legs.

Soon she has dug five or six inches into the earth. Now she digs out a walnut-sized chamber where she curls up for her winter's sleep. She has sealed herself into the chamber with the soft tailings of her digging which now fill the tunnel. Another cycle of nature is complete.

Chapter Two

The Humble Bumblebee

The English called our giant furry bee the humblebee for much of their written history. Shakespeare speaks of the humblebee in several of his plays. "The honey bags steal from the humble bee," he has Titiania Queen of the Fairies direct her fairies in *A Midsummers Nights Dream*, "and for night tapers crop their waxen thighs and light them at the fiery glow worms' eyes." It was not until the early years of the twentieth century that the name bumblebee came into common usage.

I have been unable to find an authority who claims to know the origin of the name humblebee. It may be one of those common words that evolved so long ago that its origins are forever lost in the mists of time. If I were to guess, I should think that like so many words in so many languages, its roots are in Latin. The bumblebee is essentially a ground nesting creature and the Latin word for ground or on the ground is humilis. The long Roman occupation of England may well have added humblebee to the language.

Whatever the origin the name humblebee feels just right for this furry and comfortable resident of my garden. I am not sure when or why we changed the name to bumblebee. A student of the gradual changes in language might well spend some time on the question. Sometime after the 1912 publication of F.W.L. Sladen's classic *The Humble Bee*, the change was made. The scientific world, and the entire English-speaking world, now use bumblebee as the common name of our friend.

I have used humblebee in the title of this book not only for the alliterative value of the sound and for the feeling that the name evokes for me, but, in a sentimental way, to preserve for at least a few more years the knowledge of its ancient name.

Its true scientific name carries some pleasant sound qualities as well. *Bombus!* what an appropriate name for the genus. *BOMBUS.* Whenever I hear the word I think of the full-throated roar of the engines of those lumbering, fully loaded bombers of my youth during World War II. Seemingly ponderous and slow, they were capable of carrying great loads for long distances: strong and durable all-weather flyers, just like the bumblebees.

The word *Bombus* comes from the Latin meaning a buzzing sound. The very sound of the word recalls other words: bombastic meaning high sounding, large without meaning, magniloquent, inflated. The name and its modern meanings don't do justice to this hard working, diligent homemaker but *bombus,* the old Latin name, seems to fit nonetheless.

The bumblebee joins all of the other bees, the wasps and the ants to form that large insect order, *Hymenoptera,* which has more than 100,000 described species. The name *Hymenoptera* comes from the Greek and means membrane wing (hymen = membrane; pteron = wing). The order shares in common two pairs of membranous wings, the forewings larger than the pair behind. In flight the wings hook together by a row of small hooklets lying along the leading edge of the hind wing and engage a fold in the trailing edge of the forewing.

Bees are further defined as belonging to the suborder of *Hymenoptera* called *Apocrita.* The distinguishing feature here is the possession of a "wasp waist," the constriction between the first and second segments of the adult abdomen. The "wasp waist" allows great flexibility of movement.

Further classification places the bees in a sub group of the *Apocrita* including ants, bees and hunting wasps. Its name is *Aculeata* and is derived from the Latin *aculeus,* meaning sword. Of course, the reference is to the sting with which the bee protects her nest and herself. The sting is a modified egg-laying tube or ovipositor. In *aculeates* the ovipositor has lost its egg-laying function and instead evolved into a sharp, hollow lance through which venom can be injected. Eggs are now issued directly from the body at the base of the sting.

It is thought that bees, who use their stings solely for defense, and are without exception eaters of pollen and nectar, evolved from the hunting wasps (*Sphecid* wasps). These wasps hunt insect prey—which they paralyze by injecting venom with their stings—to feed to their larvae. The behavioral difference of eating only pollen and nectar separate the bees from their wasp and ant cousins into the super family *Apoidea.* That grouping of the bees is itself broken down into eleven families of bees.

But we must not linger here with the wonders of insect evolution and classification, tempting though it might be. We must get back to our friends the *Bombus.* If you desire elaboration on this subject as well as a broad look at the world's bees let me recommend *Bees of the World* by O'Toole and Raw, (1991 Blandford Publishing, ISBN 008160-1992-4).

Of the eleven family groupings of bees, the *Bombus* belong to the family *Apidae* which includes all of the social bees. *Apidae* is again divided into three subfamilies: the *Meliponinae,* the *Apinae,* and the *Bombinae.* Of course the name is a dead giveaway. Bumblebees are of the subfamily *Bombinae.* But wait, there is even more. Subfamilies are divided into tribes and the *Bombinae* have two, *Eugulossini,* and *Bombini* and once again the name tells you which branch of the family tree to follow.

Finally we are there. There are but two genera in the tribe, the *Bombus* and the *Psithyrus.* Remember both of these names as you will be reading about *Psithyrus* later.

Family Tree of the Bumblebees

Order	HYMENOPTERA (membrane winged)
Suborder	APOCRITA (wasp waisted)
Division	ACULEATA (stings)
Super family	APOIDEA (eats pollen & nectar)
Family	APIDAE (social or quasi-social)
Subfamily	BOMBINAE (robust bodied)
Tribe	BOMBINI (true bumblebees)
Genus	BOMBUS and PSITHYRUS

There are many species of bumblebees in the world, perhaps more than one hundred. They occur in most parts of the world from the tropics to the icy poles, but they are most numerous in the temperate regions. In the warmer regions of the earth they tend to be found at higher altitudes. They do not occur in Africa, south of the Sahara, nor are they native to Australia and New Zealand although they have been introduced in both countries to aid in the pollination of clover. They are even found above the Arctic Circle where their life cycle may be as short as two weeks to accommodate the very brief window of summer plant blossoming.

All creatures must be very well adapted to survive and prosper in the unforgiving natural world and the bumblebee is surely no exception. Let us consider the structure of the bee. If we are considering the female, it will be larger than the male and will have six over- lapping plates or segments covering the abdomen. The plates provide some flexibility of movement of the ab- domen. The smaller male carries seven of the segmen- tal plates. Withdrawn within the tip of the female's abdomen is the sting. It is extended at will for self de- fense or battle. Like all bees, the male does not pos- sess a sword. Incapable of a sting, his only function seems to be that of procreation. He is the classic defi- nition of "a lover not a fighter."

The antennae of the females, the queen and work- ers, have twelve joints and are shorter than those of the males. Male antenna have thirteen joints and each joint is longer than those of the females, making their longer antennae one of the easy identifying marks when differentiating between males and females.

The distinctive colors of the various bumblebee spe- cies are all a result of colored hairs in their furry coat. The bodies of all bumblebees,underneath their furry pile, are black. Even the bright yellow bees have black bodies.

It takes an expert to identify the various species of bumblebees in a given area. In the Pacific Northwest state of Washington there are eighteen separate species. Each species has its own coloration patterns. While most are some combination of black and yellow and white, there are also a number of bees with reddish brown hairs. The combinations of colors and stripes are distinctive to a species. Usually the queen, her workers, and the males within the same species are marked identically.

As the bees differ in appearance, they also differ in temperament and life style. Sladen makes a reasonable division of life style differences by putting the bees in three categories: pocket makers, pollen stirrers and carder bees. The pollen stirrers store pollen in used cocoon cells attached to the comb as part of its basic structure. The pocket makers place the pollen for their larvae in waxen cells that they have added to the clusters of larvae. and the carder bees dwell generally on the surface of the ground in a nest of grass and moss that they have gathered around them.

Within each of these categories of life styles are a number of separate species. Sladen divided the English bees that he studied into eight species of pollen stirrers, nine species of pocket makers, and five species of carder bees, so called because they gleaned and separated nesting material as in wool carding.

In his descriptions of each of the British species he remarks on their particular temperaments. He variously describes *Bombus terrestris* as "most energetic" and says that "they defend the nest bravely when it is disturbed, hovering around it for some time ready to sting anything that approaches." Another species is described as "milder tempered than those of *terrestris* and seldom attack the disturber." Plath also describes the disposition of each of the American species that he catalogues.

"Regarding the disposition of *Bombus perplexus*," another researcher says, "this is the gentlest and least ready to sting of all the bumblebee species which I have had to deal with in the living condition. This seems peculiar, as *Bombus vagans*, which seems to be its nearest ally is exceedingly ferocious." The point is made. Each species has its own characteristics and personality. This can become of great interest and a fact to remember when you attempt to move a colony to your garden.

Bumblebees possess many physical adaptations which are of interest as we learn how they aid the bees in their specialized lives. Most species have very long tongues with which they probe the deep recesses of flowers searching for the filled nectaries. The tongue becomes an elongated suction tube powered by strong muscles in the head.

The nectar is pumped into the honey stomach in the bee's abdomen, itself an interesting organ that is capable of great distention due to its folded walls. The honey stomach can expand to almost fill the abdominal cavity and can carry a payload of nectar equal to ninety percent of the bumblebee's body weight.

The bumblebee tongue is much longer than that of the honeybee and gives *Bombus* a competitive advantage in extracting nectar from such long narrow blossoms as red clover, honeysuckle or foxglove. Bumblebees have almost a monopoly in harvesting from such flowers.

The tongue is a complex organ made up of a pair of sheaths called the maxillae and the labial palpi. They

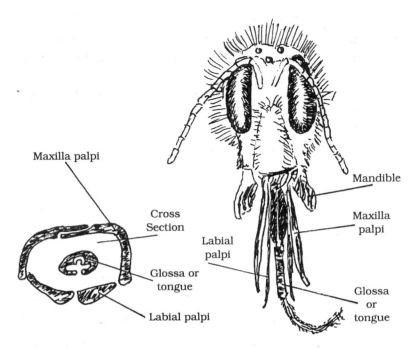

Maxilla palpi

Cross
Section

Labial
palpi

Glossa or
tongue

Labial palpi

Mandible

Maxilla
palpi

Glossa
or
tongue

Bumblebee Eating Apparatus

enclose the true tongue which is a long, hairy organ
with a groove on its underside. Nectar is sucked up
the groove when surrounded by the sheaths which, all
together, form a tube. The tongue can also be used to
lap liquids. The entire apparatus is folded up neatly
under the head when not in use.

In some species the tongue can reach a length equaling eighty-five percent of the bee's body length. Even
the bumblebees classified as short-tongued bees have
tongues reaching 50 to 60 percent of their body length.

If the short-tongued bees are unable to reach the
nectaries deep in a flower, they will often cheat by bit-

ing a hole in the blossom down near the nectaries. By inserting their too-short tongue through the hole, they can then suck up the sugar-rich nectar.

These bees are considered to be cheating because they are not contributing to pollination of the flower. Were they playing by nature's usual rules of mutual benefit, they would have entered the blossom at its opening, and in return for brushing the sexual parts of the flower with their pollen-laden body hairs, they would have been rewarded with a drink of sweet nectar. Some entomologists call the short-tongued short cut "robbery of the blossom."

It used to be thought that the pronounced buzz of the bumblebee, from which it gets its generic name *Bombus*, came from the spiracles, small holes or ports in the sides of the body. There are two pairs in the thorax and five pairs in the abdomen (six in the male). It is through these "portholes" that the bumblebee breathes.

It is now known that the distinctive buzz of the bumblebee in flight does indeed come from the beating wings, while the deep buzz that a bumblebee makes when it is irritated is caused by the vibration of its indirect flight muscles. A queen bumblebee bothered in her nest will warn off intruders with a loud and marked buzz. A clear warning not to mess with her home and brood.

Bumblebees carry pollen in "pollen baskets" on their hind legs just as honeybees do. The "pollen baskets" are in reality specialized long curving hairs which work in concert with other unique body parts to become an efficient and interesting pollen-loading and carrying system. *Bombus* can carry pollen equaling 20% of her body weight. That, in concert with a full honey stomach containing nectar equaling 90% of body weight again reminds one of those big old noisy bombers from World War II days. A huge pay-load indeed.

Corbiculum is the scientific name of the "pollen basket." It is possessed by the females only. The pollen load is carried on the outside of the tibia of the hind leg. This section of the leg is concave, bare of hair and shiny smooth. It is fringed around the edge with long, stiff and slightly curved hairs which are not plumose (branched) hairs but are smooth and rod-like.

The bee collects pollen either with its mandibles or among the hairs of its body. The hairs of the thorax and underside of the abdomen are especially good collectors as they are plumose.

Incredibly, static electricity helps in the accumulation of pollen. A flying bee builds up a substantial electrostatic charge on its body. Flowers, it goes without saying, are well grounded, especially the pollen-bearing anthers, so when the bee lands in the flower, pollen is attracted to the bee as metal filings to a magnet. O'Toole and Raw state that pollen will leap an air gap of five millimeters to attach to the bee.

Plumose Hair

Having coated herself with pollen, our busy *Bombus* now does a well-practiced grooming motion to rake the pollen from her hairs, with her two pairs of front legs, to her mouth. She then chews and kneads it with regurgitated nectar into a sticky paste. She once again grasps it with the feet and, with her middle legs, presses it to the tibia. Sladen proposes that the pressing of the pollen to the smooth side of the tibia is preceded by a complex maneuver whereby the pollen is transferred to a receiving indentation at the bottom of the corbiculum of the leg by a special brush on the metatarsal segment of the opposite leg.

Then the leg being loaded is bent and a projection, called the auricle, on the metatarsus (the next lower leg segment) rises into the receiving indentation and compresses the now sticky pollen and pushes it out onto the lower end of the corbicula, plastering it onto the mass of pollen previously collected. Finally the middle leg is used to pat down the newly added pollen parcel.

With each addition of a pollen parcel and the pressure of the auricle, the mass of pollen is moved

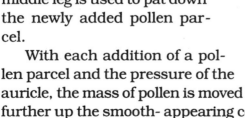
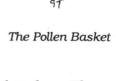

Corbicula

Receiver

Comb

Auricle

The Pollen Basket

further up the smooth- appearing corbiculum. The surrounding line of hairs bending over the corbiculum contain the mass while microscopic striations in the smooth-appearing surface run in the direction the pollen is moving. This highly complex procedure utilizes the incredible architecture of the bumblebee and makes one marvel at the specializations of nature, but the way to to truly appreciate the bee's structure is to examine it under a microscope.

As I prepare the illustrations for this book I find myself spending inordinate amounts of time glued to my microscope. Reading about the receiver at the entry end of the corbicula is one thing, but to adjust the light-reflecting mirror of the microscope and suddenly be able to see that the golden hairs of the receiver are indeed plumose (branched) is a thrill of discovery.

Eureka! Those tiny branched hairs are perfect for receiving the new load of pollen and holding it until the auricle can make its compacting sweep. The comb sits below it, ready to scrape the pollen from the leg that delivers it, perfect in its symmetry, each tooth exactly the same distance from the next, the curve of each tooth just right to rake off the pollen. The beauty and practicality of nature's creation overwhelms me and the task of communicating it in illustrations for this book is daunting indeed. My only hope is that you may have a microscope available to you. If so, find a dead bumblebee and treat yourself to looking at some of the bee parts that I am trying to describe.

The egg-laying capability of a bumblebee lies in the eight long tubes called ovarioles. These tubes emanate from a pair of ovaries and lead into a central vagina. In the tubes, eggs follow one another in progressive stages of development like beads in a long necklace. A narrow duct enters the top of the vagina from the small organ know as the spermatheca. Here the sperm received during mating the previous summer are stored until needed. Sperm is dispensed each time the queen lays an egg destined to become a female. The reproductive system opens in a small vent at the tip of the abdomen directly under the sting.

The female bumblebee is quite capable of a painful sting. Her weapon, unlike the barbed shaft of the honeybee, is smooth and easily withdrawn. The bumblebee can sting and sting again if the battle is intense, although subsequent stings have less potency as the majority of their venom is expended at the first thrust. Let me emphasize, however, that bumblebees are not by nature aggressive animals. They will sting only if their nests are under attack or they are being injured. Bees that are foraging in your garden might buzz in indignation if you bother them, but they will not attack you. Even bees bothered at their home will frequently send out a warning buzz rather than attack.

Of all the marvelous capabilities of the bumblebee perhaps the most remarkable is its ability to produce its own body heat. Insects, unlike mammals, are cold blooded creatures. This means that they must take the temperature of the world around them, that they are unable to create their own warmth and must rely on the heat of the sun.

Resting bumblebees, like all insects, have a body temperature pretty much that of the surrounding air temperature. To fly, however, the bee must achieve a flight muscle temperature of about 30 degrees centigrade. To achieve that the bumblebee shivers. The shivering of its large flight muscles, accompanied by pronounced abdominal "pumping" which circulates the warming blood throughout its body, warms the bee up to flight temperature, and allows this creature of the temperate zone to operate and thrive where otherwise it could not.

At times of marginal temperatures you can watch a bee fly to a blossom and alight to gather its pollen and nectar, but before it can take flight again for the next

blossom it must stop, shiver and pump to get itself up to flight temperature. Until the sun warms the day, it will maintain the regimen: fly to a blossom, harvest, shiver and pump, and then away to the next blossom.

The handy bumblebee even has a built-in antenna cleaner. Its antenna are vital to survival for they house the senses of smell and touch and are the organs by which the bumblebee largely senses the world around her. Keeping them clean and functional is clearly a high priority in the bee's daily life. To accomplish that necessary maintenance Mother Nature has built on to the bumblebee's foreleg a handy antenna cleaner through which the bee frequently draws its antenna to rid it of dirt, dust and pollen which might interfere with reception.

The structure consists of a semi-circular indentation in the metatarsus which is fringed with a comb of fine hairs. When the leg is flexed, a knife-like spine hinging from the tibia closes down over the indentation, forming a hole through which the antenna is frequently drawn.

A final gadget with immense utility is the wing-connecting system which must have been the inspiration for Velcro. I shall quote Sladin who quotes Bingham,

" 'the winged Hymenoptera are as a rule capable of swift and sustained flight. For this purpose they possess a wonderful arrangement (one of the most beautiful in nature) for linking together, during flight, the fore and hind wings. Examined with a good lens, the fore wing is seen to have a fold along its posterior margin, while on the anterior margin of the hind wing a row of hook-shaped bristles or hairs can easily be detected.

" 'When the wings are expanded these hooks catch on firmly to the fold in the fore wing, and the fore

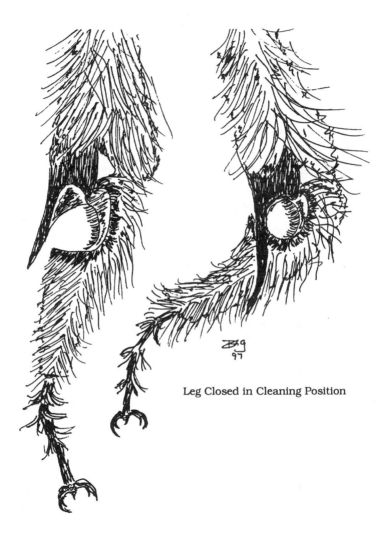

Leg Closed in Cleaning Position

Leg Straight

Antenna Cleaner

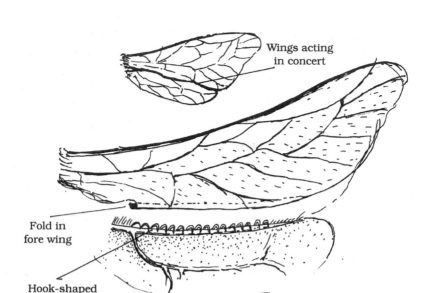

Wings acting in concert

Fold in fore wing

Hook-shaped bristles

Wing Connectors

and hind wing are enabled to act in concert having the appearance and all the firmness of a single membrane.'"

As I describe its ingenious built-in features it begins to seem that the bumblebee was designed by an industrial engineer. Surely the great evolutionary engineer is the greatest designer of all.

Sladen believed that bumblebees could not hear at all and he conducted a number of tests to prove his point. Further, he believed that their powers of sight were rather limited. It is true that they can see near objects, and that they do an orientation flight when leaving the nest for the first few times while appearing to peer intently at the entrance to the home that they are departing.

It is also true that they are experts at distinguishing flowers by their colors, but he was convinced that their sight was not outstanding and that they perceived most of their world with the sense of smell. One of his interesting observations is the intense dislike that bumblebees display for a mere whiff of the human breath. Their resentment, accompanied by an angry buzzing, is so pronounced that he cautions his readers to avert their breath and breathe from the corner of their mouth when observing a bumblebee colony up close. Studies in this century indicate that the bumblebee may have a sense of smell one hundred times more acute than man's.

Chapter Three

Bumblebee Habitat

The tragic decline in honeybee populations across North America may be a blessing in disguise for all of the native bees. The Varroa mites and trachael mites responsible for the honeybees' alarming demise do not affect the native bees. Reduced honeybee competition for the existing food supply might result in increases in the populations of the native bees, bumblebees included.

It is likely that the European honeybee, as it related to the bumblebee, was a not a beneficial immigrant to our shores. Food supplies available to bees at any one time and place are not unlimited. Because pollen and nectar supplies are finite there can be little doubt that competition for the available food occurs between the species. Competition for food with the hugely successful European honeybee must be fearsome indeed.

No one knows how the introduction of the honeybee to North America almost four hundred years ago affected the populations of native bees. The honeybees would have spread rapidly across the continent from their landing port of Jamestown, Virginia, preceding the spread of European influence to the foothills of the Rockies by many years. Apparently honeybees did not penetrate the mountain barrier and reach the Pacific shore until helped by settlers in the early 1800s.

Because of their superior social organization, and their need to store huge quantities of floral energy in the form of honey for their immense populations and over-wintering needs, the honeybees must have consumed vast amounts of the continent's pollen and nectar.

Honeybees are the superb generalists of the bee world. They live in a highly organized central village of their own construction. From it they forage in all directions to a distance of perhaps four miles, searching for blossoms, their source of pollen and nectar. When found, the scouts return to the village and signal: "I have found a fine patch of clover; I can use two hundred harvesters. Follow me." The harvesting crew leaves the village and the crop is harvested. In the meantime another scout has led a band of workers off to work a newly discovered hillside of wildflowers in bloom.

On a given day a village of European honeybees might have thirty thousand workers out in the fields harvesting. What of the poor bumblebees with their paltry colonies of twenty-five to five hundred clumsy and slow inhabitants? Will there be any food left when they get to the table? Perhaps there has always been enough for all. We aren't really sure. There was no one

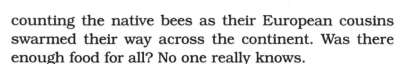

counting the native bees as their European cousins swarmed their way across the continent. Was there enough food for all? No one really knows.

Bernd Heinrich in his excellent book *Bumblebee Economics*, discusses a study of competition for pollen resources made possible by a completely unplanned ecological event of huge proportions. In 1949 DDT was sprayed over millions of acres of forests in Maine and New Brunswick to kill the spruce budworm, a caterpillar that was undergoing a population explosion potentially damaging to the pulp and paper industry of those states.

The DDT killed millions of caterpillars, but it also uprooted a natural population cycle of these creatures which saw a historic population explosion every 36 years. Once the natural cycle was broken, the DDT application was sustaining the plague of budworms because it was also killing off all its parasites and predators. Finally it was learned that the DDT was causing large bird and salmon kills and a new chemical was substituted.

Fenitrothion was then the killer of choice but this chemical is highly toxic to bees, far more so than DDT. Blueberry growers in areas near the sprayed forests immediately noticed no bees in their fields. Crops failed near the sprayed areas, and competition for pollen and nectar in the millions of acres of forest and surrounding farmlands was reduced to a minimum.

Tragic as it was, this provided a unique opportunity for an ecological experiment. Scientists Chris Plowright and Bruce A. Pendrel planted colonies of bumblebees into the sprayed area, and they compared the foraging success of those colonies with that of bumblebees operating in unsprayed forests with the normal complement of bees of all species.

The findings were dramatic. The pollen input received by the colonies in the sprayed areas exceeded those of the control colonies by a factor of five. Five times greater food gathering efficiency translates to larger bee populations, healthier bees, and better winter survival of hibernating queens.

It is at least logical to assume that the reduction of European honeybee populations will result in a corresponding increase in the populations of bumblebees and other native species. It is clearly in our interest to know more about these hardy natives and to do what we can to encourage their increase. Our assistance must be in the area of habitat enhancement so that the bees will have abundant food, secure nesting and egg-laying sites, and safe, undisturbed hibernation sites. These needs are common to all the native bees, and much can be done even in the urban back yard.

Like any creature, bees require adequate food. Most of the bees of the world are not such specialists in their feeding that they will dine at only one plant. Most of the bees that you are likely to have about your garden are opportunists and will feed at a rather large number of different blossoms, from dandelions and maple trees to the most exotic of your garden's blooms.

That is not to say that bees don't have preferences. Plant preferences differ even between the various species of bumblebees, so watch to see what blossoms the bees in your backyard seem to prefer and plant your garden with the bees in mind. Remember that they must have a constant source of floral energy every day from early spring through the darkening days of fall, so plan for continous bloom.

Included as an appendix in this book is a listing of the favorite foods of a list of thirteen North American species of bumblebee taken from the excellent book by

O.M. Plath, *Bumblebees and Their Ways*. Bear in mind that the book was published in 1934 and some of the names of plants and flowers may not be in current usage, but it should be of help nevertheless. It is also important to note that the bees listed are almost all species common to the Eastern and Northeastern states. A summer of observation and note taking will result in a much better listing for your own locality and use.

In Northwest Washington, and in my garden, I find several species of bumblebees to be eager feeders on *Pieris japonica*, raspberries, blackberries of all varieties, strawberries, blueberries, lavender, chive blossoms, cotoneaster, as well as many other plants and trees.

Beyond our backyards and gardens, the habitat needs of the bumblebees and the other native species will best be met by leaving strips and pieces of our farms and woodlands in a natural, or at least untended, state. Bumblebees and others feed on a wide variety of native plants, shrubs, and trees. Our current trend toward monocrop farming over vast areas of land does not provide the diversity of plants and blooming periods necessary to sustain a population of native bees.

Wise farmers in need of pollination of their crops will leave strips and patches of uncultivated land around and amongst their orchards and fields, even planting them with *Pieris japonica*, and rhododendrons and other proven bee feeders. The English husbandry practice of hedgerows separating their fields does this job admirably just as does the continental European practice of leaving woodlots scattered through rural areas. In France these woodlots not only provide a continous supply of firewood and wine barrels but a refuge and living space for all sorts of necessary creatures including the pollinating bees.

European Habitat

Abundant food supplies will do our bees little good without proper places for them to build their colonies and lay their eggs. Orchardists would do well to provide bee nesting blocks consisting of pieces of waste wood drilled with many holes to encourage the Orchard Masons and the various leafcutter bees. There they will set up permanent populations with subsequent generations emerging each spring to pollinate the fruit trees and surrounding crop lands.

Bumblebee populations would best be increased by leaving unmown strips of grasslands in agricultural areas or entire fields of uncut hay in areas of marginal farming utility. In these grasslands, voles and field mice build their nests, and in the spring the searching bumblebee queens will find the abandoned nests of the previous year and build their homes in the warm insulated mouse nests.

In the backyard you can foster bumblebee populations by placing dry insulating material in secure nesting boxes fitted with holes large enough for the queen bumblebee but too small for the eager birds that also seek a place to raise their young. This past summer in our garden a searching queen of the species *Bombus californicus* found a wooden bird house that we had taken down from the side of the house and stored atop a pile of firewood.

The firewood was stacked in a small structure that I had constructed with side walls of cast-off louvered shutters. The louvers provide nice air movement through the firewood stack. I had seen bumblebees lingering about the shed and several times saw them land on a louver and enter. It occurred to me that they might be returning to a nest in the woodpile within the louvers, but I never took the time to investigate further. In the fall, my wife was cleaning out bird houses and re-installing them in the various places that they occupy in our yard.

She opened the bird house that she had earlier stored with the firewood and found a nice bumblebee comb built into the grasses and feathers of the old bird nest. The nest and the large comb completely filled the confines of the birdhouse, and several of the cells neatly framed an unhatched finch egg which, for some reason, had not matured or broken. I also make houses specifically planned to meet the nesting needs of the bumblebees and will describe them in the chapter entitled "Observation Boxes."

Bumblebee nesting needs are rather simple. A secure, dark, and protected place with a small entrance, and lots of insulating warm nesting material are the essential elements. Sladen prepared nesting sites in the ground, emulating the mouse nests that he found his English bumblebees nesting in. After many years of experimentation he devised what he called his "tin domicile."

It consisted of a tin can opened at both ends. (Remember he wanted access as he was studying the bees.) He set his tins into a hole cut in the ground, covering them with removable tin lids. A long tunnel was dug down to the bottom of the tin with a special rod with a spoon-like appendage forged to the end. This entrance tunnel descended in a sloping horizontal way, and he made sure that the passageway was clear and open. A

The "Tin Domicile"

fistful of dry nesting material was placed inside the "tin domicile" and a board placed across the top of the hole for ready inspection. He had remarkable success with founding colonies in this manner as long as he built his "domiciles" on land that was not overly wet.

While I have never tried his technique, I think it would be great fun to do so. If you did not want to observe the bees, you could simply place a tin can, open end down in the hole, ream out the entrance tunnel, and cover the can over completely with dirt. The success of the experiment would be easily established by marking the entrance hole opening in some manner and watching it for bees coming and going. If I had access to a piece of empty pasture land I think I would build a number of Sladen's "tin domiciles" and see how many bumblebees I could provide homes for. Why don't you give it a try?

The final habitat need for successful bumblebee populations is an undisturbed area for the newly mated queens to build their hibernation chambers (hibercula). I know very little about the requirements of a proper hibernation site. Sladen says that while some species hibernate under the ground, others bury themselves in moss, thatch, or "heaps of rubbish," He reports that one species likes to burrow into the ground under trees while another species seems to prefer more open ground, usually the upper part of a slope facing north or northwest.

He says that it is easy to find the hibernation sites because each queen burrows into the ground, leaving a little heap of fine earth at the spot where her tunnel began. The tunnels are usually not very long, only one to three inches deep, and they are usually dug horizontally. Her hibernaculum at the end of the tunnel is a tiny chamber about the size of a walnut. He further suggests that it is dampness and not cold that the queens seek to avoid.

It seems obvious that she chooses the north facing slope because the winter sun will not heat it unduly which might cause her to awaken prematurely. The warm temperatures of the fall, shortly after she has entered her state of torpor, do not seem to waken her, but as spring approaches she becomes very sensitive to warmth and, were she on a south facing slope, might well awaken before there were any blossoms on which to feed.

Hibernating queens always enter hibernation with a full honey stomach and large fat deposits in their body for their metabolism goes on during the cold winter even though it is at a very slow rate.

I suspect there is little that you as an urban homeowner can do to provide hibernation areas in your garden or back yard. Rather you can provide food and habitat for nest building and rely on the survival instincts of the new queens, when they go searching for a home in the spring, both to find hibernation ground within flying range of your garden, and to recognize your garden as a friendly place to live.

Chapter Four

Pollination

Bees are the great pollinators of the insect world. It would be a grave omission in a book about bees to fail to address the fascinating reproductive process called pollination, for a basic understanding of the process is necessary to truly understand the role of the bees of the world.

Our friendly bumblebee is one of North America's most proficient and important practitioners of the pollinating arts and I am always alarmed and amazed when I am asked, "What do bumble bees do? What are they good for?" When I answer that they are great pollinators I frequently get a blank stare or at least a disinterested look. That all too common reaction supports the findings of poll after poll of the American public.

Most Americans do not understand the role of pollination in plant reproduction. Many of them think of pollen only as that irritating plant substance that gives

them hay fever in the spring. Yet Americans are in-
debted to the process of pollination for every third bite
of food they eat, but those who know that are surely in
the minority.

In the hope of making a small contribution to the
general awareness of this vital ecological process we
shall attempt a very much simplified description of
pollination.

The story of pollination can be described as the story
of plant sex. Floral reproduction is accomplished in a
bewildering number of ways, but at its core it is surely
a sexual event involving male and female interaction.
Through the act of pollination the fertilization of the
female ovum by the male pollen is accomplished. The
resulting cell division creates a seed which if, all goes
well, produces a new generation of the species.

The incredible story of pollination is a story of seemingly infinite evolutionary adaptations of both plants
and animals that encourage and make possible the
mutually beneficial exchange of pollination services,
on the one hand, for food, on the other. In this primal
barter the blossom attracts the animal by appealing to
its senses of sight and smell and even reproductive
ardor in some cases. Once at the blossom the plant
rewards the animal with sugar-rich nectar, protein-
rich pollen and exotic floral oils.

The animal, both intentionally and accidentally,
picks up pollen on hairs or feathers and then, attracted
to another tempting blossom, transports pollen from
the first blossom to the second. Thus pollination is
achieved, fertilization occurs, and plant sex is consummated.

Some plants are able to pollinate themselves and
are called "self pollinators," but most plants require
cross pollination. This means pollen from one plant

must be delivered to the female organ of another plant. It is cross pollination that we will deal with. It is cross pollination where the bees make their invaluable contribution.

Plant sex differs from mammalian sex in that it is consummated by an intermediary: the wind, a bird or bat or, most commonly, a bee. Mother Nature doesn't leave this vital process entirely to chance.

Highly ingenious systems of attraction and reward have evolved to improve the odds that male will meet female in the classic way. Fertilization cannot occur until one of the sexual intermediaries can be induced to transport the pollen to the blossom. Exciting sensual and practical rewards are thus advertised by the waiting blossoms.

They clad themselves in bright and colorful clothing and curtsy in the breeze in a fetching way. They send out seductive aromas of delicate perfumes to attract the intermediaries. They offer sweet and sometimes intoxicating libations and life-giving proteins in the form of pollen and exotic floral oils. All this in trade for the chance that the visitor will bring the gift of new life in the form of pollen from a distant sexual partner plant.

All the plant needs in return for this excitement and substance is the chance that a few grains of pollen from that plant in the bed across the way will brush off on her waiting stigma and trigger the miracle of fertilization. Attraction and reward, an old old story. Indeed a sexual story.

The understanding of the pollination process and the role that insects, and especially bees, play in it is relatively new knowledge. We know that ancient Egyptians realized that the date palm had to be pollinated and they did the pollination by hand. The New Testament mentions this necessity of date husbandry and Roman writings do as well, but the basic understanding of the sexual reproduction of plants and the trade of benefits between flowers and insects was only discovered in the late seventeenth century and early eighteenth century.

The discovery is usually credited to Rudolph Jacob Camerarius, a professor at Tubingen, Germany. In 1694 he published his observations in a paper entitled *Epistol A De Sexu Plantarum.* In it he postulated the male and femaleness of plants and the basic process of pollination.

The realization that bees might be providing the transport of pollen to the sexual union is attributed to an Englishman, Philip Miller. He experimented by removing the stamens from tulips in one flower bed and watching bees come from another bed laden with pollen. The emasculated tulips still were able to set lots of good seed and Miller made the connection. Miller published his observations in 1721.

In 1725 Arthur Dobbs observed in a publication of the English Royal Society, "Now if the facts are so, and my observations true, I think that providence has appointed the bee to be very instrumental in promoting the increase of vegetables."

German academic Joseph Gottlieb Kolreutes of the University of Karlsruhe demonstrated the significance of insects in flower pollination, and later Christian Konrad Sprengel, a clergyman-botanist, revealed the link between the structure of flowers and the life of the bees. He observed the nectaries and connected the bees harvesting nectar from them. In 1793 he published his classic book entitled *The Revealed Secret of Nature in the Structure and Fertilization of Plants.*

Even the great Charles Darwin got into the act and in 1876 published *The Effects of Cross & Self Fertilization in the Vegetable Kingdom.* From Darwin's day to the present the discoveries of the mysteries of plant reproduction have continued unabated. There is still much to learn.

There is immense diversity in the structure of plant blossoms but in general all flowers have a meaty stem extension called the receptacle. From the receptacle all other flower parts originate. Starting at the bottom of the flower is the tough and usually green sepal. Sepals together form the calyx and in the immature bud it is the sepals which form the outer protective bud cover.

As the bud matures and bursts open the sepals separate and curl back revealing the decorative and soft delicate petals, the colorful visual attractants in the flower's arsenal of inducements. Each petal has at its base a small receptacle for the production and storage of nectar.

This is called the nectary. It is usually covered in some manner with a flap or a lid which protects the nectar and which the bee or the bird must open to get access to the sweet stores within. The petals surround and frame the sexual parts of the flower, the stamens and the carpels.

The stamen is the male part of the flower. It is attached to the receptacle just inside of the petals. There is a cluster of stamens, each consisting of a long stalk called a filament, capped by an anther, that part of the organ which produces and stores pollen. When the flower is sexually ready, the pollen grains cover the anthers, waiting to brush off on the body of a passing bee or bird and be carried off to do their reproductive duty.

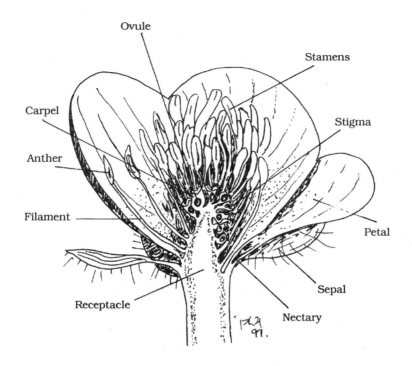

Ovule

Stamens

Carpel

Stigma

Anther

Filament

Petal

Receptacle

Sepal

Nectary

Anatomy of a Flower

At the innermost part of the blossom are the carpels, the female floral organs. They also rise from the
receptacle and stand erect, ready to catch any pollen
grains which might be brushed off onto the receptive
stigma crowning each carpel. The carpel is rather thick
and fleshy. At its very bottom each carpel contains an
ovule which, after fertilization, bears a seed.

At this point we must remind ourselves that pollination is not an end in itself. It is only the act of bringing pollen to the stigma so that fertilization can occur.
It is proper to say that the bee is a pollinator but that
pollen is the fertilizer.

The act of fertilization is indeed one of nature's miracles, for when the pollen grain lands upon the stigma it immediately begins to change. It imbibes water and germinates, producing a tiny tube. This tube grows and grows, penetrating the surface of the female stigma and working its way down the inside of the stalk of the carpel, called the style, until it reaches the ovule. The nucleus and gametes of the male pollen enter the long tube and when the tube pierces the wall of the embryo sac, the living contents of the tube are discharged into the embryo sac. The egg is fertilized and can now develop into the seed. Sexual fusion has occurred and the chance for life is granted a new generation.

It seems obvious that the weak link in this ecological wonder of reproduction lies with the pollination process. How does the pollen make the journey to the stigma? Nature cannot leave it entirely to chance; natural selection has evolved some pollination aids to improve the odds of success.

 Plants that are wind pollinated such as grasses, coniferous trees, and many decidous trees, produce prodigious volumes of pollen and literally blanket the countryside with clouds of pollen in season assuring that pollination will occur but causing no end of trouble for those folks who suffer allergic reactions to it.

 Flowers that have evolved to be pollinated by hummingbirds are usually red with long narrow petal structures which only the hummingbird can plumb. Their nectar is likely to be more liquid than insects like but just right for the diet and taste of hummingbirds.

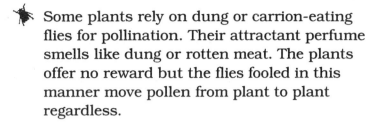

Some plants rely on dung or carrion-eating flies for pollination. Their attractant perfume smells like dung or rotten meat. The plants offer no reward but the flies fooled in this manner move pollen from plant to plant regardless.

Some plants mimic the sexual attractant pheromones of female bees to lure bees to their blossoms.

Oil-producing flowers produce fatty oils which are used by specific bees with, or in place of, nectar in the pollen mixture for their larvae. Others use oils to make waterproof cell linings. These floral oils are a rich source of energy for some species of bees.

Many desert plants bloom at night to attract the night-flying, nectar-eating bats that they rely on for pollination.

Some plants are so constructed that bees cannot get into their stores of pollen. Bumblebees and many other species have evolved a solution to the problem: buzz pollination. The bees grasp the locked up blossom from the bottom while hanging below it. Then they vibrate their bodies, creating an audible buzz, and literally vibrate the pollen grains out of the blossom onto their hairy bodies.

Bat Pollination of Saguaro Cactus

The complete story of pollination would take many more pages than we have to devote to the subject. Rest assured that our world would be sorry place were it not for pollination and it is in all of our interests to do what we can to improve the lot of pollinators on our tiny planet.

Chapter Five

Capture a Bumblebee Colony for Your Garden

Many of the students of the bumblebee first succumbed to the spell of this fascinating creature by capturing colonies in the field and transferring them to their homes for further observation. Plath writes of his childhood in Central Europe where, first attracted to the delicious honey to be found in bumblebee cells, he was soon captivated by his observations. As a result he spent a lifetime in entomology. He transferred about twenty-five colonies of six European bumblebee species to the family garden, placing them in cigar boxes where he could both partake of their surplus honey and observe their intimate activities as well.

The sixteen year old Sladen, in his charming hand-written, hand-bound booklet, *The Humble Bee, Its Life History and How To Domesticate It* devotes Chapter Four to "How To Find & Take A Nest." Can I do less?

The capture of a bumblebee colony sounds like a frightening and physically threatening task and I must confess to a certain amount of excitement every time I attempt it. However, using long proven techniques, it is remarkably easy to do. It is the one surefire way to secure a colony for observation, and it is well worth the slight risk of a sting. Of course if you are seriously allergic to bee stings this is not the sort of excitement for you.

It is important to proceed slowly, calmly, and in an unhurried manner. Not only will the bees be more easily handled, but you will do a more thorough job and collect the colony with a minimum of trauma to bees and to the all-important comb.

Choose a day that is warm and pleasant. Allocate two to three hours to the job so that you can be deliberate and savor the experience. As you will be capturing many bees that were out foraging before you arrived, you want to be sure to stay at the site long enough for all of them to return. Many colonies have only twenty to twenty-five occupants and you don't want to miss any of them as each bee is very important to the vitality of the colony.

First, you have to find a colony. It helps to network. If you tell friends and acquaintances that you will be looking for a bumblebee colony in the spring, you'll find the word spreads rather quickly. You would be amazed at what a handy cocktail party conversation piece the search for bumblebee colonies can be. Not just everyone wants to dig up a bumblebee colony. Another way to find bumblebees is to call your local police station and put your name on their list. The police are frequently called by frantic citizens who are reporting a honeybee swarm in the neighborhood. There is something about a honeybee swarm that seems to demand urgent action. Police usually keep a list of beekeepers who are only too happy to come and remove a swarm. But It is unlikely that your police have anyone on their list who will pick up bumblebees.

Another source is a list of local pest eradication services. Unfortunately they are usually the ones who ultimately deal with unwanted bumblebees in a city. They often dislike exterminating bumblebees and would be grateful to step aside for you.

If you want an excuse for a pleasant walk in the country, simply pack your collecting equipment in a pack and drive to marginal farm land in the countryside nearest you. Look for uncut grass fields with lots of old dried grass from the year before. Try to imagine where there might be lots of field mice. There is where you will find the bees. Be sure and stop at the farm house to ask for permission. Folks who live in the country may be sensitive about people wandering over their land with butterfly nets over their shoulders. I have found that permission is almost always given but never without a quizzical or amused expression.

Capturing your first colony will be an exciting experience. Here are Sladen's instructions. "Before starting out assemble your capturing kit of a strong trowel, a glass jar with wide shoulders, a water glass with a rim the same size as the rim of the jar, two cardboard covers, and two pocket handkerchiefs. If you plan on taking more than one nest you will need an extra jar and two more handkerchiefs for each nest.

"Having found a grassy and sheltered field bordered by sloping banks or woods, and having chosen a still warm day you walk slowly looking for flying bees. If a bee rises up before you mark carefully with your eyes where it came from. If you see a bee descending watch

Sladen's Method of Bee Capture

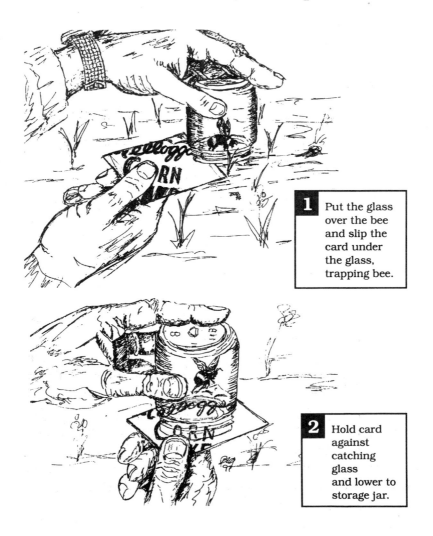

1 Put the glass over the bee and slip the card under the glass, trapping bee.

2 Hold card against catching glass and lower to storage jar.

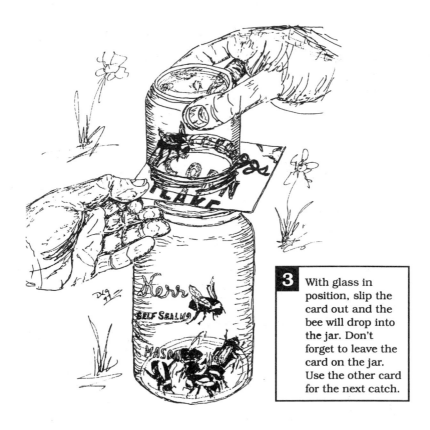

3 With glass in position, slip the card out and the bee will drop into the jar. Don't forget to leave the card on the jar. Use the other card for the next catch.

where it goes. When the nest is found look for the hole, disturbing the herbage as little as possible.

"Place the jar on level ground nearby and commence digging being careful not to fill up or lose the hole. Each bee that comes out should be caught in the glass and cardboard and transferred, mouth downwards to the top of the jar. The cardboard should then be drawn out, the concern shaken, and the bee will fall into the jar. Then slip the cover on it and proceed in the same way to fill the jar by taking more bees with the glass and the other cover.

"As you dig there are several signs of approaching the nest: more bees coming out, a very loud buzz which will be the angry queen, and finally bits of dry grass, dead leaves, or animal hair that indicate the nesting material.

"Expose the nest and gently brush away the nesting material revealing the bright yellow comb, a few young bees, and the queen rushing backwards and forwards in great agitation. The queen should be taken in the glass and cardboard and put in with the workers in the jar." Sladen says that the queen will never attack you and will only sting if you should grasp her in your fingers. "The comb can now be carefully picked up and put into the nest box that you have prepared. If there are young queens the foundress queen can be known by her large size and by the shabby condition of her furry coat. In some cases it will be entirely worn off and the queen will appear a leathery black.

"To do a through job, a small piece of comb should be broken off and left in the cavity from which the comb was lifted. In half an hour's time it will be covered with returned foragers which can in turn be bottled and added those bees you have already captured.

"The jar is then inverted onto the second handkerchief which is tied snugly around it to be transported home. The comb is placed into a suitable hive or nest box and at night the now drowsy bees can be shaken into it. In the morning the flight hole of the hive is opened and the bees rapidly adjust to their new setting."

Sladen states that he has taken hundreds of colonies by this method and that it works admirably. If you are worried about being stung he elaborates on nest-taking in his mature book published in 1911 and states that he took "nearly a hundred humble-bee nests and did not receive a single sting."

He emphasizes that the important point is to catch every bee that comes out of the nest and not to disturb the bees in the nest until nearly all have been captured either coming or going. If a bee does escape now and again it is not likely to attack unless it is one of the really fierce species and even they seem to have more courage only when several of their nest mates have also escaped. He does suggest, however, that if the bees pour out of the nest it is wise to beat an immediate retreat.

I have used Sladen's method and it works like a charm. I've learned that if the jar has a constricted neck the bees will not rise out of the jar when the cardboard is briefly removed. With some species the emerging bees will turn over on their backs raising their legs in a defensive posture. These can quickly be picked up by offering them a corner of the cardboard to grasp and then shaking them off into the jar.

My only improvement on his system is to take along a small ice chest with a bit of ice in it. When the jar is filled with the bees, place the jar in the ice chest. The bees will soon become comatose and can easily be shaken into the waiting nest box after the comb has carefully been set into the nesting chamber. With the entrance hole plugged with a cork the colony can now be transported. The bees will return to normal very quickly when they warm up and will soon be busily restoring order to their comb in its new surroundings. In the morning the flight hole of the hive is opened and the bees rapidly adjust to their new setting.

His final caution is to protect the comb with its precious brood of larvae and pupae from crushing, and from extremes of heat or cold. Being away from their doting queen and workers for several hours should not harm the comb's occupants. He also suggests you take only the comb and not the surrounding nesting materials as parasites and predators are probably occupying the nesting material and the colony will be better off settled in new material of dried grass and moss or upholsterers cotton.

Plath also devotes a chapter in his book to the finding and collecting of bumblebee colonies. He reports that he has the best hunting on plowed but not harrowed land which has been lying fallow for several years, or during the haying season. Just as soon as the grass near a bumblebee nest is cut, the worker bees returning from the field are disoriented and will often betray the opening to the nest by their frantic searching. Remember, the bees memorized the appearance of the growth at their nest entrance. The mowing machine has changed the appearance of their world.

Plath's youthful method in dealing with a surface nest was to get a large cigar box in one end of which he drilled a flight hole of a size that could be stopped with a cork. Proceeding to the nest site he picked up the nest with both hands and quickly placed it in the cigar box. He then replaced the nest, now in the cigar box, to the place from which it had come, pulled the cork from the flight hole and departed, letting the activities of the colony return to a semblance of normal. At dusk, when almost all the foragers had returned to the nest, Plath himself returned, corked up the cigar box and transported the entire colony back to his family garden.

He confesses that this system worked nicely for surface nests, but digging up a subterranean nest resulted in frequent and severe stingings. Plath must have been a courageous lad.

In the summer of 1921, now wiser or less bold, he adopted Sladen's methods of colony taking with some minor modifications. His book offers several suggestions for making the task easier. He suggests that the bees are less pugnacious in the hour just before sunrise. (He doesn't mention how you see to do the job.) Also, he keeps track of the direction of the tunnel by inserting a pliable stick or root into the nest hole to be sure of not losing the tunnel to crumbling dirt as he digs. Finally he suggests that if the tunnel branches, a sharp whack on the ground above with a spade will usually send a couple of angry workers out of the branch that leads to the nest. After you have caught them and put them into the jar you will know which branch to continue digging.

The final capture method which I wish to describe is that shown to me by Lynn Royce, my entomologist friend from Corvallis, Oregon.

Lynn's capture kit consists of an insect-collecting net such as can be purchased for five or six dollars at any children's toy store; a cardboard box containing a large collection of the plastic 35mm film canisters with their snap-on lids; a small ice chest with a modest load of crushed ice; and, finally, a closable container of wood or cardboard in which to transport the comb to its new home.

On my trip to Oregon I carried one of my newly designed and manufactured bumblebee houses: THE HUMBLE BUMBLE HOME, complete with two compartments, a clear plastic observation lid, the covering wooden lid, and, of vital importance, a number five cork to plug up the flight hole.

The colony of *Bombus californicus* occupied an abandoned mouse nest tucked into the middle of a woodpile of oak fireplace wood standing in an open yard
near Corvallis, Oregon. Lynn and I, with our butterfly
nets ready, stood beside the woodpile watching for bees
coming or going. This method takes a little patience,
but surely not more than does duck hunting, or even
waiting for a city bus.

About every five minutes a bee would arrive and do
a few circles around the mouse nest. One of us would
catch it in a net, take the net to the ground and reach
into its folds with a film canister in hand.

Pinning the bee against the netting and slipping
the open film can over it was an easy task once I got
onto it. It helps to have a flat and smooth surface to
place the net upon like a piece of plywood, or a side of
a cardboard box. Once the bee is inside the film can
and being held against the netting and the flat cardboard surface, slip the plastic lid over the film can and
snap it into place. Then simply place the bee on the ice
in the ice chest so that it can cool off and will not hurt
itself battering its wings against its prison.

In my own capture kit I have punched small air
holes in the film canisters fearing that the bees might
suffer from lack of oxygen, but Lynn's experience
doesn't indicate that that is necessary. Probably the
bees' oxygen needs are sharply reduced by the cold-
induced torpor that they rapidly fall into.

When all of the incoming and outgoing bees had
been captured and sent to the cooler we removed the
logs on top of the nest and gently placed the comb in
the brood chamber of the HUMBLE BUMBLE HOME.
Unfortunately we found the queen dead at the entrance
to the nest.

Lynn had observed the colony the day she called me to drive down and collect it. She had thought it a strong and healthy colony, but we deduced that the occupants of the home on the property had sprayed the nest that night. The beautiful black and yellow queen lay dead at her doorway with a number of her workers at her feet. There was evidence of the spray about them.

Sad as it was, we were delighted to find the comb clean and beautiful, apparently protected by its enveloping mouse nest from the poisonous spray. There were three huge queen cells as well as many other larval and pupal cells in various stages of development.

Lynn and I sat at the woodpile in the warm summer afternoon, discussing the unfortunate ignorance of mankind in the ways of the bumblebee, and waiting for any straggling foragers to return. When convinced that there were none, we put the cork in the flight hole of the HUMBLE BUMBLE HOME, and, one by one, opened the film canisters, gently shaking the cold and torpid bees onto the soft upholsterers cotton upon which we had placed the yellow comb.

Lynn gently placed several of the bees in the palm of her hand and blew her warm breath over them until they began to stir. Then, dropping them into the HOME, we replaced the clear viewing lid and watched as the bees slowly returned to activity. Immediately they returned to their brood to resume their doting care of the pupae within. I replaced the wooden lid, giving them the security of darkness, and the colony was ready for its long trip back to Bellingham.

Chapter Six

The Observation Hive

One of the great pleasures you can get from capturing a bumblebee colony is to observe it in an observation hive. Your pleasures are increased many times over if your observation hive is installed inside your home and the bees are free to come and go to the outside through a connecting tube between hive and window.

In the previous chapter I described removing a bumblebee colony from a woodpile, and installing it in an observation box or "hive." I transported the bees and the brood comb over three hundred miles to my workshop. There I measured and cut a board to just fit in my opened window sash. I then drilled a hole in the

board to accept a short piece of plastic 3/4 inch water pipe. Setting the
observation model HUMBLE
BUMBLE HOME on a shelf
in front of the window, I
marked with a pencil
where the pipe
touched the
"HOME." I then
drilled a match-
ing hole in the
"HOME" and in-
serted the other
end of the pipe
into it. With a
four inch long
pipe I had con-
nected the bumblebees
to the outside world. They could now come and go at
will.

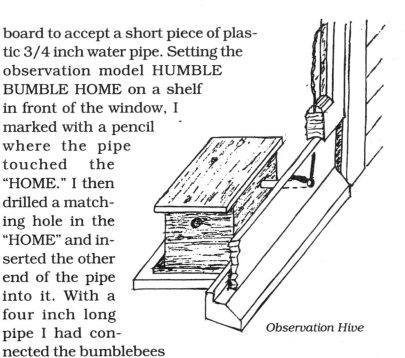

Observation Hive

Before I made the connection, however, I removed
the board from the window sash and, with a black
marking pen, made a bold V shaped mark at the entrance hole to aid the bees in finding the entrance to
their new home. I also nailed to the board, just below
the entrance hole, a tiny landing platform should the
bees need something to light on before crawling into
the hole.

The connection made, I rushed outside and anx-
iously waited, and watched. Within sixty seconds the
first worker burst from the entrance hole. To my joy
and amazement she immediately started her orientation flight. Turning to face the hole from which she
had just come, she made a circular flight of perhaps
two feet from side to side. Her next circle was several

inches wider, and with ever-widening circles she pro-
grammed her memory to be sure that she could return
to her family. Finally she had achieved a thirty or forty
foot swing and she wheeled away.

Soon another worker emerged and repeated the
performance as I stood there in awe. Each bee that
emerged repeated the orientation routine, and now I
was left to wonder if they would really find their way
back. Imagine my pleasure when the first bee returned.

I could not decide whether to wait for them outside
the building where I could enjoy their finding of the
hole, or whether I wanted to be inside the building peering through the clear acrylic sub lid watching the bee
come out of the tunnel, through the vestibule chamber
and directly through the hole in the dividing wall onto
the comb.

I got nothing accomplished that first morning after
my trip to Oregon, I could not bear to leave the bees.

Peering into the inner chambers of a bumblebee
colony is to watch a caring, thrifty, and industrious
family at work. Some bees scurry here and there with
great purpose, intent upon a mission that I cannot quite
calculate, but surely one that is important to the bee.
Others extend their bodies and, with languid maternal
care, drape themselves over the bulging pupal cells.
With gently pulsing abdomens they concentrate their
warm blood to flow through their abdomens so that
the pupae will be warmed and comfortable. Yet others,
the outside foragers, enter through the tunnel entrance,
clamber over the vestibule and through the inner entrance to rush to the waiting honey pot. There they tip
their heads into the wide mouth of the pot and con-
vulse their abdomens to add their payload of nectar
into the communal pot. Then on they go to the waiting

pollen storage vessel to scrape the golden treasure from the "baskets" on their legs.

Here a black and gold worker carries brown wax from an abandoned storage pot to add to the roof canopy being built over the comb. There another is seen descending through the maze of silken cells to the lower regions of the comb, finally disappearing from my sight into the catacombs on some unknown mission. Mysteries abound as one peers into the bumblebee's home.

Little wonder that they have so captivated those who have studied them. I have yet to watch a queen lay her eggs or build her waxen egg cradle. I have not seen the invasion of the "Usurper Queen" and watched the drama of that long truce, always ending with the mortal battle and the death of the founding *Bombus* queen. The adventures that lie before me, and you, if you will avail yourself of an observation hive, are boundless but imagine what these adventures can mean to the children in your life.

Involve a child in your exploration of the bumblebee world and together share one of the great stories of the natural world.

Chapter Seven

Psithyrus, The Enemy Within

Now begins a tale of almost Shakespearean drama, about a visitor to the castle who first befriends the queen, then finally slays her and usurps the crown, reducing all of the dead queen's subjects to slavery in the service of the usurper's family. It is the story of that close relative of the *Bombus*, the *Psithyrus*.

You will remember that in Chapter Two we learned of the two genera which shared the tribal name *Bombini*. They were the genus *Bombus* and the genus *Psithyrus*. They are cousins. They look almost alike, yet one is like the cuckoo, a wastrel and a vagabond. While the *Bombus* side of the family labor diligently caring for their children and their homes, that queen of the ne'er-do-well side of the family, the *Psithyrus*, lurks about awaiting the opportunity to move in with her cousins and freeload an existence.

The *Psithyrus* queen waits until her *Bombus* cousin has her home well established, with lots of healthy workers and pollen stores in the cellars below. Then she comes calling. She is a friendly guest for a few days, lulling her *Bombus* queen hostess into complacency. Then she attacks, and because of her heavier armor and murderous intent, always succeeds in killing the *Bombus* queen. Soon the docile *Bombus* workers forget their slain queen mother and devote themselves to the service of the usurper *Psithyrus* queen. The *Psithyrus* lays her eggs and they are fed and tended by the *Bombus* workers. The duped *Bombus* work just as diligently and effectively for the interloper and her brood as they did for their own, but now they work to raise future murderers of *Bombus* colonies in future generations.

There are a number of separate species of *Psithyrus*, each victimizing specific species of *Bombus*, so that, for example, *Psithyrus insularis* will prey on only *Bombus flavifrons* and no other. The *Psithyrus* are very similar in appearance to the *Bombus* but can be differentiated by the fact that the females lack the pollen-carrying corbiculum on the hind legs. Their hind legs are hairy. They produce no workers and only produce the sexual males and queens which will carry on their perfidy. The parasitic *Psithyrus* always closely resemble the *Bombus* species that they prey on so if the *Bombus* host has a red tail, so will the *Psithyrus* that victimizes it.

Sladen, in describing *Psithyrus rupestris* which is parasitical to *Bombus lapidarius*, reports that her wings are dark brown, not clearly transparent as in her victim, and her flight is feeble, producing a lower sound than that of her victim because the rate of wing vibration is slower.

But the great difference between murderer and victim is the exceedingly hard and thick exo-skeleton of the *Psithyrus* which covers it like a coat of mail and assures her of victory in her inevitable battle with the host queen. The segments of the abdomen in particular are very hard and lap tightly against one another as there are no wax-producing glands between the segments. It is very difficult for the *Bombus* queen to force her lance between them and strike a mortal blow. In addition, the *Psithyrus* has a sting that is a better queen killer, stouter and more curved than that of the *Bombus*.

Psithyrus's movements are lethargic and awkward and when visiting flowers for food she is clearly not as industrious or successful as *Bombus*. Why should she be? She will soon have willing slaves looking after her every need. She spends the pleasant summer days using her sense of smell to search out a nest of the particular *Bombus* species that she is destined to victimize.

The usurper queen wants to find the nest of her victim shortly after the first several batches of workers have emerged, for these early workers are less hostile to strangers than the hosts of stronger workers in a more established nest. Sladen reports finding dead *Psithyrus* queens at the entrances of strong colonies of *Bombus terrestris*. The dead invaders were completely denuded of hair, and around their bodies lay fifteen or so dead *Bombus terrestris* workers, mute testimony to a fierce battle.

In a weaker nest the *Bombus* queen will greet the invader with initial hostility but fall short of an outright attack. Soon she will retreat and sulk. The

Psithyrus, however, treats the queen with indifference. In the first few days she ingratiates herself with the *Bombus* workers and soon they cease any hostility towards her. Even the queen seems to grow accustomed to her presence. Finally the *Psithyrus* queen seems more lively, more in charge, taking a growing interest in the comb, while the *Bombus* queen, perhaps dimly aware of her fate, becomes listless and lethargic.

Suddenly the usurper attacks the brooding *Bombus* and in an unequal struggle forces her sting between the foundress queen's armored abdominal segments, administering a lethal dose of venom into the soft tissue between the plates. The assassination is complete, the queen is dead, long live the *Psithyrus* queen say the *Bombus* workers as they begin their labors as her subjects.

Very soon after ascending to the throne, the *Psithyrus* begins to lay her own eggs, and why not, you might ask. She has a pleasant castle with adequate stores. She has a healthy retinue of eager *Bombus* servants with many replacements being tended in their egg, larval and pupal stages. Now all the new queen need do is tend to the future of her own family. She will lay no worker eggs; she has the *Bombus* to do the work. Her eggs will all be either new queens or males who, after a proper upbringing by their *Bombus* nursemaids, will go out into the world to mate and provide for the survival of their species into another spring.

Chapter Eight

Barbarians at the Gate

A gruesome fate awaits all bumblebee colonies. If they are not raided and destroyed by a marauding skunk or a whole host of insect and animal enemies, most of them finally succumb to a host of parasites that inhabit the lower recesses of the comb or the surrounding nesting material.

Plath describes seeing crows dining on a surface-nesting bumblebee colony that they had found in a grass field. He is sure that field mice, voles and other rodents consume their share of bumblebee brood. He also describes in great detail the techniques of the skunk in devouring bees, brood, and honey stores of several colonies while he watched.

If the colony can escape such a sudden and traumatic end, it will surely fall into a slow decline as the

foundress queen's energies and egg laying capability begin to wane and the onset of fall reduces the supply of pollen and nectar available to the hive.

Then the colony's defenses begin to falter as the accumulation of parasites grows. The colony harbors various intruders. Some are only scavengers feeding on the castoffs of the castle. Some, however, are deadly assassins eating not only the wax and the pollen stores but the larva and pupae themselves.

Many of the assassins are the larvae of various flies, some are the larvae and the adults of beetles, one of which, Antherophagus, invades the colony in a unique way. The adult beetles frequent flowers such as hydrangea and hollyhock. There they lie waiting with open mandibles. When the bumblebee arrives to feed, they grasp its tongue, or a leg or antenna, and ride the bee back to the nest. In the nest the beetle meets another of its kind but of the opposite sex. They mate and the female lays her eggs in the deserted cocoons or debris in the lower regions of the comb.

A common and destructive nest intruder is the larvae of the wax moth which dines not only on the comb but the brood itself. These active and aggressive larvae appear in great numbers in almost all failing colonies and finally consume resources and brood faster than the tiring bumblebees can replace them. Finally the exhausted queen and the few survivors among her retinue seem to give up, just sitting upon their crumbling castle waiting for death. The genetic future of this colony rests entirely with the success next spring of those new queens who now sleep peacefully in their Hibernaculums somewhere under a cool grassy slope.

Bumblebees don't succumb to the barbarian throngs without a determined fight. The invading skunk is well stung for his trouble. A bird consuming a

bumblebee must be very adroit to avoid the bee's lance.
Plath relates an amusing incident of a single bumblebee, in the defense of its nest, chasing several cackling
young roosters around and around in the chicken yard.

At least one bird, how-
ever, specializes in preying
on bumblebees. The
fierce insect eater,
the Northern
Shrike, thrives
by perching on a
high vantage
point from which
it swoops down on
passing bumblebees. If
the bird is sated, it stores
its future meals by impal-

The "Butcher Bird"

ing its victims on thorns or barbed wire fences. These
macabre displays are not uncommon in the bird's range
and have earned the grisly bird, not without reason,
the name "Butcher Bird."

Intruders that enter the subterranean tunnel leading to a bumblebee nest are often turned away or killed
in a staunch defense by guards apparently stationed
at the entrance. It is well documented that at least one
species of bumblebee, *Bombus fervidus*, coats some
invaders with a sticky substance which the workers
apply, drop by drop, from their mouths. It is probably
nectar from their honey stomachs. The victims of this
sticky attack are rendered helpless or at least slowed
down. They are then stung to death. The victims of the
Bombus fervidus sticky treatment are invariably creatures possessing superior strength or sting capability.
Intruders of lesser capability are simply stung to death
or slain with the bumblebee's stout mandibles.

An interesting and common defense technique is employed by workers or bumblebee queens. When they are suddenly touched or threatened, they raise one of their middle legs in a threatening fashion. If the annoyance continues they will lift a second leg on the same side of the body, and finally will turn over completely on their back. In this position they will remain for a minute or more with mandibles wide open and the tip of their abdomen curved upward. If you are foolish enough to reach down and touch the bee, she will grasp your finger with her mandibles and her legs and administer the sting. If you wish to collect her you can offer a cardboard, or a stick and she will usually grasp it long enough for you to pick her up and place her in a container.

Sometimes bumblebee colonies are attacked by ants attracted to the colony's honey reserves. Wasps have also been known to attempt a robbery from time to time. Internal and external parasites of all descriptions also afflict the bumblebees, causing illness and debilitation to those so victimized. All in all the life of the bumblebee is not an easy one, yet this robust and thrifty creature survives.

Unfortunately even its chief beneficiary, mankind, is one of the bumblebee's worst enemies. We plow up its nests in the fields or cut them up while mowing the hay. In our ignorance and fear we stock our groceries and convenience stores with insidious poison sprays to use on any colony of bees that we see with little or no thought to their value, either to ourselves or to the natural world. Undaunted, the sturdy humblebee returns each spring to usher in a new season of warmth and blossoms,and, with its customary good humor, repays our transgressions by pollinating our shrubs and berries, our fields and gardens.

Chapter Nine

Bumblebees for Your Garden

Bumblebees are a wonderful presence in your garden. You can increase your chances of having a healthy population of these beautiful creatures in any number of ways. First, you must plant those shrubs and flowers that will attract and hold the bees in your space. To learn what works best in your local area simply spend some time during spring and early summer with a notebook, jotting down the names of those plants that attract the bumbles. A planting of those flowers and shrubs will reap great dividends in furry pollinators in the years to follow.

The second way is to provide nesting habitat for the bumblebees. Sladen's "tin domicile" technique would be a fun experiment. A simple nesting box like my HUMBLE BUMBLE HOME filled with soft and insulating nesting material is a powerful attractor for a foundress queen in search of a home. Bird houses that are not cleaned out each season will also attract the bees. Insulation exposed in a building wall or stuffed in a tin can thrown in the corner may attract the bees. I have seen them nesting in such manmade habitats as a pile of cut sod with nice spaces between the sods.

Piles of grass clippings or a well-dried pile of leaves will work. Remember that the bee's nesting requirements include a mass of soft and dry insulating material that they can dig into, while leaving an entrance tunnel that can be protected. Bumblebees want a cool environment where they can supply the warmth and regulate the temperature. Put nesting boxes on the north side of buildings or in the shade as too much heat will kill the young bumblebees.

When a wandering queen shows interest in your nesting box or pile of grass clippings, you must not disturb her until she has truly set up housekeeping. A bumblebee queen is very sensitive to interruption until her larvae have spun their cocoons and entered the pupal stage. If she is disturbed prior to that point she is apt to abandon her nest and her investment in time and effort up to that point and simply leave, never to return.

A perfect example of this was found at the home of my daughter and son-in-law, the home of my grandchildren Evan, Annie and Laura. The family had mounted a birdhouse on a north facing wall on the second story porch. The bird house had been occupied in previous years by a family of English sparrows. It was easily reached from the porch. Annie and Laura noticed a large bumblebee entering and leaving the one inch entrance hole. Their healthy curiosities aroused, the girls rapped gently on the bird house and were immediately answered by a loud buzz resonating from the cedar structure.

This exciting response was reported promptly to Mom and the rapid buzz was demonstrated for her. Then the bird house was left alone. They concluded that a bumblebee was establishing housekeeping there and didn't want to be disturbed.

In subsequent days no activity was seen at the birdhouse and the matter was almost forgotten in the busy summer activities of five- and- eight year old girls. In mid-October as my daughter read the first manuscript of this book she was reminded of the experience and, curiosity aroused, removed the birdhouse and brought it to me for inspection. We pried off the back and found the house to be about one-third full of old bird nest: dried grasses, moss, torn pieces of paper and plastic, bits of feathers—and one tiny bumblebee honey pot.

The bumblebee queen of the spring had clearly made her nesting cavity and constructed the honey pot, but the girls' curious rapping unnerved her and she left for more private accommodations.

The surefire method of getting bees to live in your garden is to employ the capture-and-move-techniques set out in Chapter Five, but whatever method you use I hope you will find renewed pleasure in watching the bumblebees in your neighborhood as they go about their busy lives. Do what you can to make their lives easier and to tell others what you have learned and what you will observe.

While you watch the bumblebees, watch for the other native pollinating bees: the leaf cutters, the masons, the ground nesters, the stem nesters. There are more than four thousand separate species in North America alone. There is bound to be an incredible number of species of bees where you live. Watch for them, protect them, and they will reward you with fruitful gardens and orchards and a peaceful heart.

THE END

Bibliography

Alford, D.V. *The Life of The Bumblebee.* London: Davis-Poynter Limited, 1978.

Buchmann, Stephen L., and Gary Paul Nabhan   *The Forgotten Pollinators.* Covina, CA: Island Press, 1996.

Crompton, John   *The Hunting Wasp.* Cambridge, MA: Riverside Press, 1955.

Essig, E.O.   *Insects of Western North America.* New York, NY: The MacMillan Company, 1926.

Fabre, J.H.   *The Mason Bees.* Garden City, New York: Garden City Publishing Company, 1925.

Heinrich, Bernd   *Bumblebee Economics.* Cambridge, MA: Harvard University Press, 1979.

O'Toole, Christopher, and Anthony Raw   *Bees Of The World.* London: Blandford Press, 1991.

Plath, O.E.   *Bumblebees and Their Ways.* New York: The MacMillan Company, 1934.

Proctor, Michael, Peter Yeo and Andrew Lack   *The Natural History of Pollination.* Great Britian: Timber Press Inc, 1996.

Sladen, F.W.L.   *The Humble Bee.* Herefordshire, Great Britain: Logaston Press, 1889 and 1912.

Stephen,W.P., G.E. Bohart and Philip F. Torchio.   *The Biology and External Morphology of Bees.* Corvallis, OR: Oregon State University, 1969.

Stephen, W.P.   *BumbleBees of Western America.* Corvallis, OR: Oregon State University.

Buchmann, Stephen L.   *Buzz Pollination in Angiosperms. Handbook of Experimental Pollination Biology.*

Appendix A

Some Favorite Bumblebee Foods

Bombus affinis: rhododendron, barberry, horse chestnut, mountain laurel, rose, St. John's wort (*Hypericum*), larkspur, jewel weed (*impatiens*), butter and eggs (*linaria*), milkweed, sumac, buttonbush (cephalanthus), sweet pepperbush (clethra), and boneset (eupatorium)

Bombus terricola: willow, crocus, gooseberry, barberry, rhododendron, mountain laurel, honeysuckle, rose, white clover, basswood, purple vetch, milkweed, basswood, sumac, sweet pepperbush and boneset.

Bombus bimaculatus: willow, crocus, buffalo currant (ribes aureum), pedicularis, diervilla, rhododendron, mountain laurel, honeysuckle, red clover, purple vetch, basswood, pickerel weed, purple loosestrife.

Bombus impatiens: crocus, pieris, rhododendron, barberry, mountain laurel, rose clover, purple vetch, pickerel weed, purple loosestrife, buttonbush, jewelweed, beggars ticks, goldenrod, burdock and asters.

Bombus perplexus: rhododendron, mountain laurel, raspberry, basswood, honeysuckle, buffalo currant, yellow-wood (cladrastis litea), sweet pepperbush.

Bombus ternarius: willow, pieris, rhododendron, rose, red clover, basswood, purple loosestrife, sweet pepperbush, eupatorium, and golden rod.

Bombus vagans: rhododendron, honeysuckle, pedicularis, mountain laurel, diervilla, red clover, purple vetch, baptisia, boneset.

Bombus separatus: rhododendron, pedicularis, buffalo currant, rose, red clover, purple vetch, basswood, milkweed, purple loosestrife.

Bombus rufocinctus: frequents flowers similar to those visited by *B. auricomus* and *B. separatus*.

Bombus borealis: diervilla, honey locust, yellow-wood, larkspur and purple vetch.

Bombus americanorum: diervilla, rose, honey locust, red clover, purple vetch, larkspur, St. John's wort, red clover, purple vetch, baptisia.

Bombus fervidus: pea tree (*caragana*), buffalo currant, rose, red clover, honey locust, purple vetch, larkspur, pickerel weed, butter and eggs.

About the Author

Brian Griffin came upon his fascination with our native bees late in life. A native of Bellingham, Washington, educated at Whitman College, Griffin has always been intrigued by the natural world. He spent his childhood summers among the woods and tide pools, and his falls fishing and hunting with his father. Natural History classes in college, and many years of sailing the Pacific Northwest made him a keen observer of nature.

His introduction to the Orchard Mason Bee in 1986 began an avocation which in his retirement has resulted in two books—*The Orchard Mason Bee* (now in its 2nd edition) and *Humblebee Bumblebee*—and a growing business selling bees and their nesting supplies across the United States.

He is a sought-after speaker on his subject of native American bees and has spoken at The Philadelphia Garden Show, the Pacific Northwest Garden Show, The International Conference of Master Gardeners, and many other venues.

Griffin still lives in Bellingham, Washington, with his wife Marya. Retired after 35 years in business, he is busy in his second career.

Buy Knox Cellars Native Bee Products

You can buy a Humble Bumble Home, a starting population of Orchard Mason Bees, or other related items described in this book from selected garden centers and nature stores across the country.

Contact Knox Cellars for a list of our dealers near your home, or for our mail-order catalog, if you do not have a Knox Cellars dealer nearby.

Knox Cellars Native Bee Products

- Orchard Mason Bees in paper liners
- Orchard Mason Bees in wooden slices
- "System" nesting tubes
- "System Nester"
- "Nester Liners"
- Nester Shelter
- Shelter Extensions
- Wooden nesting blocks for three types of native bees
- "The Gift of Pollination"
- "Build a Bee House" kit
- *Humblebee Bumblebee*, by Brian Griffin
- *The Orchard Mason Bee, 2nd Edition*, by Brian Griffin
- *Bees of the World*, by O'Toole & Raw
- Video, *The Orchard Mason Bee*
- Audio cassette *The Orchard Mason Bee*
- "Humble Bumble Home," bumblebee nest box
- Bee Watcher's Notebook
- Bumblebee tee shirts
- Orchard Mason Bee tee shirts

Knox Cellars Native Bee Pollinators

1607 Knox Ave.
Bellingham, WA 98225
Tel: (360) 733-3283
Fax: (360) 733-3283
Email: brian@knoxcellars.com

25724 NE 10th St.
Redmond WA 98053
Tel: (425) 898-8802
Fax: (425) 898-8070
Email: lisa@knoxcellars.com

Please visit our website: www.knoxcellars.com

Field Notes

Field Notes

Field Notes

Field Notes

Field Notes

Field Notes

Field Notes

Field Notes

Field Notes

APPENDIX B

A Field Guide to North American Bumblebees

We hope that you will use this field guide to better acquaint yourself with the bumblebees that frequent your garden.

You will find that the observation of bumblebees and the other native bees, like bird watching, will heighten your powers of observation and add immensely to your awareness of the world around you.

Identification of bumblebees, however, is a difficult task. Many species have several subspecies which exhibit different color patterns. Many species tend to have variations in their own standard color patterns. To further confuse the observer, males frequently have color patterns different from the queens and workers.

This guide displays the most common coloration of the queen of the species. Happily, the workers of most species adopt the color patterns of their queen, so when you identify the worker you have identified the species.

You might find it useful to take notes of your bumblebee observations in the field and then take those notes to the field guide for identification at your leisure. Trying to thumb the pages of the guide while watching a flying bee is very difficult.

You will find it helpful to draw a diagram of a bee, showing head, thorax and abdomen with six segments. Sketch in the bee's color pattern onto the diagram. Later you can use the field guide with more deliberation.

Keep notes of the first appearance of the queens. Note the date you first see the workers. Later you can note your sightings of males and new queens.

The identification of one of the *Psithyrus* species is a special event and surely worthy of notice in your field notebook.

We have given a general indication of the size of the species, however, the ultimate size of any bee is determined by its nutrition in the larval stage. Thus there can be large variations in size within a species.

Perfect identifications are possible only by experts who utilize differences in wing veining and various minute body parts to distinguish one species from the others.

Don't let the difficulty deter you from the fun of observation and identification. Maybe you will become an expert.

Bumblebee Structure

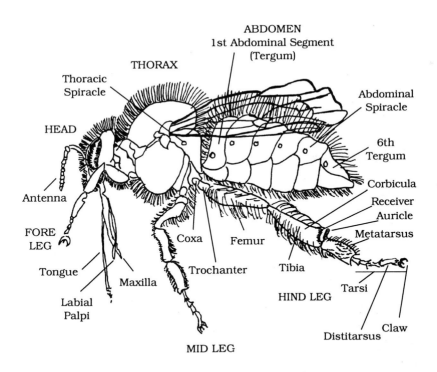

THORACIC
Thoracic
Spiracle

THORAX

ABDOMEN
1st Abdominal Segment
(Tergum)

Abdominal
Spiracle

HEAD

6th
Tergum

Antenna

Corbicula
Receiver
Auricle

FORE
LEG

Coxa   Femur

Metatarsus

Tongue

Trochanter   Tibia

Maxilla

Tarsi

Labial
Palpi

HIND LEG

Distitarsus   Claw

MID LEG

The Bombus of North America

Bombus affinus:
Large bee, rear half of abdomen is black, forward half, orange-yellow, thorax yellow, head black. Que., Maine entire N.E. south to Ga.,N.C., West to Mont.,Colo. Appears mid Apr. until Oct. Large colonies to 200 members. Gentle disposition. Preyed upon by Psithyrus ashtoni.

Bombus appositus:
A medium sized bee almost identical to B.borealis except head and front of thorax are yellow instead of orange. Abdominal black tip is smaller. B.C. ea. to Sask., so. to N.M., Ariz., & Cal. Cascade and Sierra Nev. Mtns. Seen mid March to mid Sept.

Bombus balteatus:
A large bee, mostly yellow with a black head. A circular black spot on top of thorax, wing to wing,. A black band across the fourth abdominal segment. A bee of arctic Alaska and Canada. also south down the continental spine of North America to the Sierra Nevadas of California and high mountains of N.Mex.

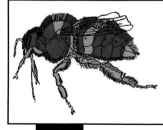

Bombus bifarius bifarius:
Medium size bee. Mostly yellow including yellow head. Large black patch on back of thorax, wing to wing. Front of abdomen is black as is tip of abdomen. A narrow black stripe bisects the abdomen at the second segment. Found in the dry inland parts of B.C.,Ida., Ore., Utah., Cal. They emerge in late April and are seen until the end of August.

Bombus bifarius nearcticus:

Medium size bee with a yellowish-white head and thorax. Thorax has a strong black spot on top between the wings. The abdomen is mostly black with yellow at the first segment and in a narrow band at back of the last segment. Rather common bee in western America. B.C., Wa., Ore., Cal., Ida., Utah. Seen from late April to early Sept.

Bombus bimaculatus:

Medium size. Abdomen is black except for 1st segment which is yellow. Thorax is yellow with a black spot at top of thorax between the wings. Black head. Seen mid Apr.to early Aug. Life cycle is very short. small colonys, perhaps 80 bees.nasty disposition. Ont.,entire East coast west to Dakotas, Kansas, Okla., Miss.

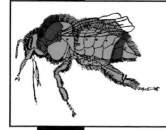

Bombus borealis:

A large bee. distinctly yellow and orange alternating stripes except for a black stripe wing to wing across the top of its thorax and the black tip of its' abdomen..S.Canada from No.Scotia to Alta. Nor.U.S.,Maine to N.J. and west to Montana. Appears late in spring. Late May to Sept.

Bombus californicus:

Large bee almost identical to B. vosnesenski except the head is black.Heavy black pile covers the bee with the exception of a bright yellow cape at front of thorax and the yellow abdominal stripe. B.C., south to Cal., Ariz., and N.Mex., Mexico. Late April to late August. Constant color patterns.

Bombus caliginosus:

Small size. Yellow head and front of thorax. Black from rear half of thorax to tip of tail except for a thin yellow stripe near rear of abdomen. Tip of abdomen is black. Almost identical appearance to B. vosnesenskii but smaller in scale.Late March to mid August. Coastal Wa. Ore. & Cal but not as far north as Puget Sound.

Bombus centralis:

Small bee. Black at the very tip of the abdomen, then broad orange stripe. The remainder of abdomen and thorax are yellow except for a black spot atop the thorax. Yellow head. B.C. & Alta. so. to Cal

Bombus crotchii crotchii:

Large size, mostly black but with yellow on front of thorax. A broad band of yellow across the abdomen. black tail. restricted to California,Ariz., Baja Cal, & northern Mexico.

Bombus edwardsii:

This is a small bee, mostly yellow. It has a yellow head and thorax with a black stripe on top stretching from wing to wing. There is a broad black band across the abdomen and a black tip. Ore.,Cal.,Nev.,Ariz.,no. Mex. seen from early March to Sept.

Bombus fervidus fervidus:

Medium size bee, entirely yellow except a black head, black thorax stripe wing to wing, and small black tip of abdomen. Que., and N.B. So. to Ga. West to B.C., Wa., Ore.,Cal., & no. Mexico. Seen from mid March thru mid Sept.

Bombus flavifrons dimidiatus:

This is a small bee. Has several coloration patterns depending on locale. Yellow head, yellow thorax with black spot on top, mostly yellow abdomen has two black stripes and a black tip. Some bees have more defined black plus a black dorsal stripe connecting the black rings on top of the abdomen. So. B.C., to Cal.

Bombus flavifrons flavifrons:
This is a medium sized bee with orange on the last two abdominal segments and a small black tip. The front of the abdomen is yellow. Thorax is yellow with a prominent black spot on the thorax top. A western bee found from Alaska south to Cal., Ariz., & N.Mex.

Bombus fraternus:
Large bee, mostly yellow, black head, black tail,(last 3 segments), black stripe across top of thorax,from wing to wing. Found from N.J. to Fla., west to N.Dak., S.Dak.,Nebr., Colo., N.M.

Bombus frigidus:
Medium sized bee, mostly yellow, yellow head. Large black wing-to-wing stripe on top of yellow thorax. One abdomenal segment is black making a bold black stripe across the yellow abdomen. Tip of abdomen is apt to be slightly rufous. Alaska & N.W.T. So. along continental divide to high elevations in Colo.

Bombus griseocollis:
Large bee, entire thorax is yellow. black head. the first abdominal segment is yellow and the rest of the bee is black. Sometimes called B.separatus Que. south to Fla., west to Wa. Found east of cascades in B.C, Wa., Ida.,Ut., Or. and Williamette valley to No Ca.

Bombus huntii:
A small bee, Yellow head and thorax with a black patch on top of thorax. Abdomen is predominately orange with some yellow and a small black tip. B.C. & Alta So. Cal, Utah & N.M. Seen April thru end of Sept.

Bombus hyperboreus:
A large bee, mostly yellow but black on last three abdominal segments and on the head. Also a black stripe across top of the thorax wing to wing. Found in arctic Alaska, Canada, and Greenland.

Bombus impatiens:
Medium size, black on abdomen behind the 1st segment which is light yellow-white. thorax is light yellow-white. Head black. April 15th tru Oct 15th. Entire East Coast west to Mont, Wyo.,Ut.,Ariz.,Kans. ground nesters, very populous, over 500 in colony, pretty nasty disposition.

Bombus lucorum lucorum:
Large size, black head, yellow shoulder patch on front of black thorax. Front segment of abdomen yellow, black center stripe across abdomen. White tail with black tip. Alaska So. to southern B.C.,Alta.,Yukon, & N.W.T.

Bombus melanopygus:
A striking small bee. Pale yellow thorax with grey spot on top. Abdomen is Rufous-orange with a black tip. Found in greatest numbers along the coasts of Ore.,Wa.,and B.C. Also in N.Cal.,Ida.,Alaska, northern Rocky Mtn states. From sea level to 8,000 ft. Seen from mid April to mid September.

Bombus mixtus:
A small bee, mostly yellow but a black thorax spot, one thin black abdominal stripe and a small black tip at the tail. Alaska, so. to Cal., Ida., & Colo. An early flier, seen in March to early Sept.

Bombus morrisoni:
Large bee. entirely yellow except for black tail. Widespread in the west.tends to occupy arid areas of Ca., Ida., Ut., N.M., Ariz., Colo., Wa., B.C., S. Dak., Nebr. Seen early April to mid-Sept.

Bombus nevadensis auricomus
Large size, black head, yellow on front of thorax, black abdomen with a broad yellow band across abdomen, tail black. Found on East Coast from Ont. to Fla. West to Tex, Okla, Colo., Wyo.,Mont. Also Sask., Alta.,& B.C.

Bombus nevadensis nevadensis:
Large bee, mostly yellow with black head, black tail, black spot at top center of thorax. some black at very front of abdomen. Alaska So. to Cal. East of the Cascades and Sierras,although found on Vancouver island and Oregon's., Willamette Valley, B.C.,Ida.,Utah.,Nev.,Ariz., N.M., Wyo. Seen from late Apr. to late Sept.

Bombus occidentalis:
A large striking bee with black head, bright yellow cape at front of thorax, black thorax and first three abdominal segments. rear segments of abdomen are white, sometimes with a yellow stripe on the third abdomenal segment, then black again before the white tail. Occupies most of western America and common in lower B.C. and Pacific Northwest states of Wa.,Ore., also in Ida., Mont., Colo., Utah. Appear in late March.

Bombus pennsylvanicus pennsylvanicus:
Large bee, black head. Yellow in front of thorax, rest of bee black except for a broad yellow stripe across the abdomen. Que., Ont., Nebr., Colo., N.M., and Mexico.

Bombus pennsylvanicus sonorus:
Large size, mostly yellow, but black head, black stripe across top of thorax from wing to wing. and black at tip of tail. Texas west to California and Mexico.

Bombus perplexus:
Large size, entire thorax yellow, black head, abdomen is black except yellow on top of front part of abdomen and a thin yellow stripe just before its black tail. Emerges in Apr. nests in May, workers seen last week of May. Last seen mid August. Populous species, subterrainian nester. Gentlest of the bumblebees says Plath. Alaska to Maine and south to Wisc, Ill, Fla.

Bombus polaris polaris:
Large bee. Mostly yellow except black head, black abdominal tip and a large black spot on top of the thorax, wing to wing. An arctic bee whose range circles the arctic pole, arctic Alaska, Canada, Greenland, and Eurasia.

Bombus rufocinctus:
Medium size, red-orange abdomen with black tip. Forward part of abdomen (ist segment) is yellow as are the head and thorax. There is a black spot in top center of thorax from wing to wing. This is a gorgeous bee. Nests in walls of buildings and boxes. common on West Coast, found across northern tier of states to East Coast N.C.,N.B.,and Que. Many color variations. a testy disposition around nest.

Bombus sandersoni:
Small bee, mostly yellow with black head, black spot on top of thorax. Black tail with a rufous tip. Ont., to Newf., So. to N.C. and Tex.

Bombus sylvicola:

A small bee, yellow, black and orange. Head is yellow, black spot on top of yellow thorax. Black tip of abdomen. Bold orange stripe across yellow abdomen. Alaska to Newf.and south on the high mountain ranges of cascades, Sierra Madres and Rockies to Ca., Nev., Utah, & N.M. Seen early June thru late Sept.

Bombus ternarius:

Medium sized bee with a wide band of rufous-orange on its abdomen bordered by yellow. The very tip of the abdomen is black. The thorax is yellow with a broad band of black across the top of the thorax from wing to wing. Appears only in British Columbia's high central plateau. Its bright red orange stripe fades quickly after emergence to a pale orange. Queens appear in late April and last until late August.

Bombus terricola occidentalis:

Medium-large bee, black head, yellow cape at front of thorax then all black thorax and abdomen back to the fourth and fifth abdominal segments which are yellow, then a thin black stripe and finally a yellow or red tail tipped with black. Alaska So. to no. Cal.,Nev.,Ariz., N.Mex., and S.Dak.

Bombus terricola terricola:

Medium-large bee,black head,yellow cape at front of black thorax. Orange-yellow-white abdomen with narrow black stripe at fifth segment. tail is yellowish white.East coast So. to So.Car. West to continental divide and north well into all Canadian lower provinces. Preyed on by Psithyrus ashtoni. Nasty disposition when nest is bothered.

Bombus vagans vagans:

Small bee, yellow with black tail and black head. Very shaggy pile. Northern tier of states from coast to coast. South to Ga., Tenn., includes Wa., Ida., Mont. Emerges in May. good candidate for box nesting. Gentle disposition. Preyed upon by Psithyrus laboriosus

Bombus van dykei:

Small size, similar to B. caliginosus but yellow abdominal stripe is a bit farther forward. Not abundant. Found from Wa. to Cal.

Bombus vosnesenski:

Large bee, mostly black except for yellow head and shoulder area on front of thorax and a thin yellow stripe at rear of abdomen. This is one of the most wide spread of bumblebees in the west. B.C., so. to Cal., Nev., Mex., Baja Cal. Late April to Late August. constant color patterns.

Bombus sitkensis:

Small size, black and weak yellow. Head and thorax are yellow except for large black patch atop thorax. Abdomen is yellow with broad black stripe. Alaska, so. to Cal., Ida., Mont., & Wyo. Seen March to end of Sept.